MUIRFIELD
AND THE HONOURABLE COMPANY

WILLIAM ST. CLAIR OF ROSLIN
Captain 1761, 1766, 1770 and 1771

MUIRFIELD
AND THE HONOURABLE COMPANY

GEORGE POTTINGER

SCOTTISH ACADEMIC PRESS
EDINBURGH AND LONDON
1972

PUBLISHED BY
SCOTTISH ACADEMIC PRESS LTD.
25 PERTH STREET, EDINBURGH EH3 5DW

Distributed by
Chatto and Windus Ltd.
40 William IV Street
London WC2

First published 1972

ISBN 0 7011 1872 5

Printed in Great Britain by
R. and R. Clark Ltd., Edinburgh

To the wives
who appreciate the virtues
of the Honourable Company

CONTENTS

ILLUSTRATIONS

IN COLOUR

IN MONOCHROME

NOTE: The photographs of Henry Cotton and Gary Player are reproduced by kind permission of the *Glasgow Herald* and the *Evening Times*.

FOREWORD

by the Honourable Lord Robertson
Senator of the College of Justice
Captain of the Honourable Company 1970-72

During a visit to Florida over thirty years ago I was asked to play golf at Tampa and was allotted as caddie a small Southern boy of about twelve years of age. After watching my practice swings apprehensively for a few moments, he enquired anxiously: 'Have you played before?' I replied that I had. Clearly puzzled, his next question was: 'Where are you from?' I replied that I was from Scotland. This puzzled him even more, and, after some consideration he asked: 'Have they got a golf course there?' I replied that they had a golf course there. His final question summed up his total disbelief: '18 holes?'

International communications have improved since then (though my swing has not), and lovers of golf everywhere know something of the history and traditions of the Royal and Ancient Golf Club of St. Andrews, the premier club and law-giver for the whole game of golf. But few will be so well acquainted with the equally remarkable story of the Honourable Company of Edinburgh Golfers, which now has its home at Muirfield. With a continuous existence since 1744, and promulgator of the oldest set of Rules of Golf, the Honourable Company is descended from the 'Gentlemen Golfers' who played at Leith Links from at least the fifteenth century.

The Honourable Company transferred from Leith, first to Musselburgh, and then in 1891 to Muirfield, at that time a stretch of open country beyond Gullane in East Lothian, some nineteen miles from Edinburgh. Here, in privacy and anonymity, apparently with little forethought and almost absent-mindedly, the Club laid out, and has developed over the years, what is now by universal acclaim one of the greatest golf courses in the world.

The Honourable Company is a private club with 680 members, and Muirfield is its own property. As the readers of this book will discover, it regards golf as a social, and sociable, game, and match-play as the true and proper expression of golf. But, while maintaining to the full the traditions and rights of its members, and their privacy, the Honourable Company, as owner, also fully accepts that it is, as it were, trustee for Scotland – and for the world – of its great links. It is proud and privileged to accept the staging of the premier golfing tournaments – the Open and Amateur Championships, the Ryder, Walker and Curtis Cups – from time to time.

Scotland is a small country, but Scots like to think that it has given many of the good things of life to the world – and not least the healthy, friendly and wholesome game of golf. The Honourable Company is the home of the Foursome – sometimes called the 'Scotch' Foursome – and regards it as the true game, the epitome of all that is best in golf. A prominent Notice hangs beside the entrance to the clubhouse at Muirfield, saying: 'Fourball games are forbidden at weekends and on public holidays'. Any member (or visitor) who attempted to break this rule would get short shrift. And, if it be retorted that a player plays twice as many shots in a fourball game as in a Foursome, the Muirfield man would reply – 'Play 36 holes in $4\frac{1}{2}$ hours (as we do) and you will get the same number of shots, twice the exercise, far more fun, and you won't have to wait between shots. Furthermore you will learn to play golf better.'

The bicentenary of the Honourable Company fell in 1944; because of the War no celebration of the occasion was possible. Otherwise this book would probably have been written at that time. It has now been made possible primarily by the devoted research of Colonel T. R. Broughton, a former Captain, who has laboriously ploughed through all the vast quantity of written records in the Club's repositories – Minute Books, Bett Books, plans, letters and other documents. The help given by I. H. Bowhill, a former Recorder, and by that great Scottish golfer and golf writer S. L. McKinlay, who read the book in manuscript and contributed much wise advice, is gratefully acknowledged.

The writer, George Pottinger, has such affection for Muirfield that he now lives in a house which he has built beside the first fairway (at a point, the cynics say, where he can retrieve balls hooked by wild drives from the first tee). He is a fearsome putter and a formidable opponent in a Club match, and I would strongly advise that no one should agree to play a Foursome against him for any stake at all without mature consideration and a skilful partner. But, to be serious, he has in this book exercised a careful and fastidious choice in his pruning and sifting of the history of the

Honourable Company. And, above all, in his writing he has finely caught the humour, the fellowship, the tradition and the ethos of the Club.

In this Open Championship year (1972) there will be many visitors at Muirfield, from all over the world. I hope that they will enjoy their visit, for Muirfield is 'a place that likes to be visited'. I hope that they will read this book and absorb something of the atmosphere, the standards, the friendliness and the spirit of the place. Above all, I hope that they will find and mark what I believe to have been the essence of golf in Scotland as it has been played since 1681, when the future King James chose as his partner in an important match (a Foursome, of course) against the English, one John Paterson, 'a poor shoemaker'. Golf in Scotland is a national game, a game of the people. It is the ultimate democratic game, the great leveller and humbler, and the game of true worth, in which 'a man's a man for a' that'. In this game a man must be self-reliant, and hard work, concentration and self-control are the true virtues.

In the early eighteenth century, it was said of the golfers at Leith Links – 'the greatest and wisest of the land were to be seen . . . mingling freely with the humblest mechanics in pursuit of their common and beloved amusement. All distinctions of rank were levelled by the joyous spirit of the game . . .'

Though times have changed, and less attention is rightly paid to artificial distinctions today, I like to think that this spirit of universal good fellowship and respect for the worth of all men is inherent in the love of golf in Scotland; and in particular that it is part of the spirit and tradition of the Honourable Company.

Muirfield, 1972

CHAPTER I

THE ANCIENT AND HEALTHFUL EXERCISE

Golf is a Scottish game. Whatever conclusion is drawn from agreeable academic disputes about its origins, there is no doubt that the first unmistakable historical reference to the game of golf is found in a decree of the Scottish Parliament dated 1457. Nowhere else has the sport been practised with such zeal since then and Scots have always been its leading missionaries at home and abroad. For golf it can be claimed, as the Royal Caledonian Curling Club arrogantly asserted for one of Scotland's other national games, that its introduction 'into countries furth of Scotland has always been the work of Scotsmen. While other nationalities have readily taken up the game, its progress has chiefly depended on Scotsmen.'

Golf is also – with due reverence to the many fine courses in Ayrshire and the West – primarily an East Coast game. The geology of our island is such that links made of sand which has ceased drifting and has acquired a covering layer of turf are to be found in greater abundance on the Eastern seaboard than elsewhere. The steep, serrated coastline in the West contains fewer sandy beaches.

So this is a book about golf played in the East of Scotland successively through the centuries on links at Leith, Musselburgh and Muirfield. It relates the story of the Company of Gentlemen Golfers which eventually became the Honourable Company of Edinburgh Golfers. It is about the customs adopted by the members and the changing attitudes to the game. Great figures, from the merciful Lord President Duncan Forbes of Culloden, 'patron of the just, the dread of villains, and the good man's trust', to William St. Clair of Roslin with his scarlet coat and closed stance, and Robert Maxwell, the most engaging of champions, appear. But, first, a few practice swings at golf's respectable ancestry.

There is no agreement about the circumstances in which golf – the simple practice of yielding to the natural impulse to strike a small moveable object with a stick – is first recorded. Some Stone Age warrior, swinging

a club to flex his biceps for more lethal purposes, may have played the
first stroke. Thereafter it survived as one of the exercises which, according
to Bertrand Russell, sublimate the combative instincts.

For those who would prefer a classical origin, there is the Roman school.
There are references in Latin to *pila lusoria pluma facta*, a ball made of
feathers for playing games. Martial also refers to *pila*, to *follis*, apparently
a hollow ball, and to *paganica*, which is alleged to have been a popular
Roman sport. *Pila paganica* may, accordingly, be proposed as the first
designation of our own royal and ancient game.

But only the more credulous will accept the theory that golf was brought
to Britain by the Roman legions. This fanciful proposition commended
itself to two erudite historians. The Rev. John Kerr was one of the first to
propound it in his *Golf Book of East Lothian* (1896). The Reverend sportsman found time to write not only a mammoth compendium on golf but
also an equally extensive history of curling: a tribute both to his pro-
ductivity and the lightness of his pastoral duties at Dirleton. More recently,
Sir Guy Campbell in the admirable *History of Golf in Britain* (1952)
supports the theory that, just as the British took cricket to India, the native
Scots learned *pila paganica* from centurions anxious to relive the tedium of
garrison duties on the Walls that marked the frontiers of empire. The
proof of this theory would admittedly make for historical continuity, but
the prospects are at least dubious. Aerial photographs may perhaps reveal
the outlines of an early, now overgrown and hidden, Roman links some-
where on the Scottish Border. But, without supporting archaeological
witness of this kind, the Roman case lacks credibility. As a corollary to the
Roman theory, during the last world war members of the Honourable
Company on duty with the Eighth Army in Italy found, as they made their
dusty way to Rome, a well-appointed course on the edge of the Via Appia
Antica with fairways pointing straight towards the dome of St. Peter's.

Then there is the Continental school where the evidence is mainly
pictorial. The Flemish Book of Hours (1500–20), now in the British
Museum, contains an illuminated page said to have been decorated by, or
under the control of, Simon Bennink, which appears to portray an early
contest. Certainly there are four players, three armed with clubs, three
balls and a hole. There are also a number of Dutch paintings of slightly
later date showing games being played, on land and on ice, with primitive
clubs. 'Het Kolven' was the Low Countries' name for golf, and the most
significant painting is the great 'Frost Scene' by Van de Velde (1668) which

WILLIAM INGLIS
Captain 1782–84

shows two kilted players taking part in a foursome on ice. Here it is easier to agree with Sir Guy Campbell that they may have been Scottish refugees during the troubled times of the Stuart wars.

But real authenticity requires recourse to the Scottish records. There had admittedly been some reference to 'cambuca' played with a curved club from the time of the English Edward I, but the statute of the Scottish King James II in 1457 leaves no room for doubt. So popular had the game become, at the expense of more immediately practical exercises like archery, that the defence of the realm required an ordinance that:

> Fute-ball and Golfe be utterly cryed down, and not to be used. . . .
> And as tuitching the Fute-ball and the Golfe, to be punished be the
> Barronis un-law, and gif he takis the un-law, that he be taken be the
> Kings officiars.

A further decree of 1471 showed that King James III was equally clear that 'Fute-ball and Golfe be abused in time comming'. And, to complete the picture, James IV in 1491, under the peremptory heading 'Fute-ball and Goulfe forbidden', ordered that:

> In na place of the Realm be usit fut-bawis, goulf or uthir sik unprofitable
> sportis.

The stern decrees afford a splendid example of the Scots' perverse habit of forbidding themselves to do what they want to do. Possibly no one but the Scots would develop the game and promptly deny themselves the pleasure of playing it under pain of statute. A masochistic impulse also apparent in their attitude to the licensing laws. Only in Scotland is the elixir distilled which, in Neil Gunn's words, 'makes manifest the works of creation and leads the basest man to bless his enemy'. But there are many places where it is easier to satisfy a reasonable thirst.

A few years later, however, in 1502, James IV signed a Treaty of Perpetual Peace with England; defence requirements seemed no longer paramount; and he was himself recorded as buying clubs and balls and paying a forfeit for losing to the Earl of Bothwell. James V played at Gosford, and Mary, Queen of Scots, at Seton – both in East Lothian and only a few miles from Muirfield. The Union of the Crowns in 1603 extended the field of play. Golf was one of the national habits that James VI and I took south with him and it is not surprising that the wisest fool in Christendom should have been the first to see the dangers of imported equipment. In 1618, because 'no small quantity of gold and silver is

B

transported zeirly out of his Hienes' Kingdom of Scotland for buying of golf-balls', James Melville, along with some friends, was granted a twenty-one year monopoly for supplying balls and authorised to imprint 'ane particular stamp of his awin' on them.

Golf was now endemic and the general impression to be derived from contemporary records suggests that the links at Leith must have been the most popular. The account books of Sir John Foulis, Bart., of Ravelstone (in the Publications of the Scottish History Society, 1894) are full of entries about golf there:

1672		*Scots*
Feb. 14	Spent at Leith at Golfe	£2. 1. 0
Feb. 26	„ „ „ „ „	£1. 9. 0
Nov. 19	Lost at Golfe with Chancellour Lyon, Master of Saltoune, etc.	£5.16. 0.

Sir John must have been rather wild off the tee on that November day for, in addition to losing his wager, he had to pay another twelve shillings for golf balls.

The Duke of York, later James VII and II, when he stayed at Holyrood House as High Commissioner to Parliament, played often on Leith Links during the 1681–82 season. An otherwise unidentified Mr. Tytler of Woodhouselee recalled that, in his youth, he had –

often conversed with an old man, named Andrew Dickson, a golf club maker, who said that, when a boy, he used to carry the Duke's golf clubs, and to run before him and announce where the balls fell.

Dickson is the first recorded forecaddie.

The Duke is also credited with arranging the first international match. Wisely choosing as his partner John Paterson, a poor shoemaker who, according to Robert Clark in his *Golf* (1893), 'was not only the best golfer of his day, but whose ancestors had been equally celebrated from time immemorial', the Duke beat two English noblemen whose names have not survived. A victory of much profit for Paterson who built a house in the Canongate, Edinburgh, with his reward from the Duke. The family crest emblazoned on the wall suitably displayed a hand grasping a golf club beneath the motto 'Far and Sure'.

Records for the next few decades are sparse until 1742 when Alexander Elphinstone beat the otherwise infamous Captain Porteous of riot fame before a crowd large enough to attract notice. Some significance had been seen in the happy partnership of royalty and trade at the Duke of York's International, and the increasing social spread of the game is endorsed in the eloquent words of the *Statistical Account of Scotland*:

> the greatest and wisest of the land were to be seen on the Links of Leith, mingling freely with the humblest mechanics in pursuit of their common and beloved amusement. All distinctions of rank were levelled by the joyous spirit of the game. Lords of Session and cobblers, knights, baronets, and tailors might be seen earnestly contesting for the palms of superior dexterity, and vehemently but good-humouredly discussing moot points of the game, as they arose in the course of play.

Golf at Leith Links – and at St. Andrews and Perth – was becoming more popular every year, but there was as yet no sign of any corporate body or collection of individuals forming a club or society to promote their common interest in the game. The establishment of the Company of Gentlemen Golfers in the 1740s seems to have come from the golfers' habit of taking refreshment at a particular tavern after their exercise. The Gentlemen Golfers were accustomed to meet for this laudable purpose at Luckie Clephan's tavern at Leith. Clephan was an innkeeper and clubmaker who died in 1742 and it was the house of his widow that became the Company's first headquarters. While it can be only conjecture, it seems probable that the moving spirit behind the formation of the Company was Duncan Forbes, Lord President of the Court of Session.

Duncan Forbes's significance in Scottish history stretches far beyond the Company of Golfers. From his powerful office he was strenuous in trying to prevent the 1745 Rising, and in the unhappy aftermath he tempered justice with an abiding mercy. As a reward for doing the state some service, he was granted the unusual, and extremely acceptable, privilege of distilling whisky at the Ferintosh distillery free of excise duty. Years later, the vigilant eye of the Exchequer lighted on this apparent anomaly. The privilege was withdrawn, to give rise to one of Robert Burns's most heart-searing lyrics:

> Thee, Ferintosh, O sadly lost!
> Scotland, lament frae coast to coast!
> Now colic grips, an' barkin hoast
>   May kill us a';
> For loyal Forbes' charter'd boast
>   Is ta'en awa!

But it is perhaps as a golfer that Duncan Forbes would most wish to be remembered. It was said that his passion for the game was such that, on the few days a year when frost or snow made the Leith Links unplayable, he would be seen belabouring his ball along the sands of the seashore. And what better example of restrained parental pride than his account of a match with his son?

This day after a very hard pull, I got the better of my son at the gouf. If he was as good at any other thing as he is at that, there might be some hopes of him.

The Company was fortunate in its association with Duncan Forbes. He died two years after the Rising, on 10th December, 1747, and was fittingly described as 'a patriot without ostentation or pretense, a true Scotsman with no prejudices, an accomplished and erudite scholar and a man of genuine piety'.

After a year or two of meeting at Luckie Clephan's, the golfers evidently felt the need for some more formal recognition, and on 7th March, 1744, the Edinburgh Town Council, in response to applications which had been made from time to time by 'several Gentlemen of Honour skillful in the ancient and healthful exercise of the Golf', presented a Silver Club to be played for annually according to the 'proper regulations' drawn up by the desire of the Magistrates by the 'Gentlemen Golfers'. The Town Council seem to have regarded the Gentlemen Golfers as a body that could be recognised. The Honourable Company of Edinburgh Golfers accordingly claim as their birthday 7th March, 1744, and the Minute of the Town Council which provides the documentary evidence of the Club's existence marks the beginning of their written records. They have been kept ever since and form the oldest continuous record of any Golf Club in the world.

The first Minutes of the Club and the records of the Town Council prescribe the regulations for conducting the competition for the Silver Club and the Rules of Golf to be observed on the Links.

Play for the Silver Club was to take place annually on the Links at Leith and the victor was to be styled 'Captain of the Golf' and be given power to determine all disputes touching golf and golfers. An unusual occasion of law-making power being conferred for athletic prowess. A further condition was that the winner should append to the Club a gold or silver coin or ball. This has been done ever since by the Captain of the Honourable Company, although successors to that eminent office are not now elected entirely for their skill on the links. There was to be an entry fee of one crown to go to the Victor who, in turn, would

> at the receiving of the Club give sufficient caution to the Magistrates and Council of Edinburgh for fifty pounds sterling for delivering back the Club to their hands one month before it is to be played for again.

There are now three Silver Clubs, all presented by the City of Edinburgh, in possession of the Honourable Company. Two have their full complement of balls given by Captains, and the third is nearly complete. Although the Honourable Company has long been at Muirfield, outwith the City boundaries, and before that at Musselburgh, the ties between the City and the Club remain close. The match between the Corporations of Edinburgh and Glasgow is from time to time played at Muirfield, and the Lord Provost is on occasion received as an honoured guest at one of the Club Dinners.

The last Regulation, stipulated by the Town Council, declared that:

> upon no pretence whatsoever the City of Edinburgh shall be put to any sort of expense upon account of playing for the said Club annually except to intimate by Tuck of Drum, through the City, the day upon which it shall be annually played.

It is not known how long this martial ceremony was continued, but presumably it lapsed on the departure of the Honourable Company to Musselburgh in 1836.

When the first competition for the Club was played on 2nd April, 1744, the entrants were:

Duncan Forbes	David Dalrymple
Hew Dalrymple	James Carmichael
George Suttie	William Crosse
John Rattray	James Leslie
Robert Biggar	Richard Cockburn
James Gordon	James Veitch

Duncan Forbes did not actually play but competed the following year.

Of these twelve apostles, the winner was John Rattray, Surgeon in Edinburgh, who became the first 'Captain of the Golf'. Since, at this stage, the only entrance qualification was the payment of the five shillings fee, Rattray has some title to recognition as the first of all Open Champions.

Rattray won the Silver Club again in 1745, but thereafter his golf was interrupted by less pleasurable activities. In the early hours of an autumn morning that year he was called out of bed to act as Surgeon to Prince Charles Edward's troops at Prestonpans. From there, although, it is said, somewhat reluctantly, he accompanied the Prince both on the march south to Derby and on the withdrawal to Culloden where he was taken prisoner. Only the intervention of his fellow member, Duncan Forbes, saved his life, and in 1747 he was released to reassume office as Captain. Despite these disagreeable experiences, Rattray was able to enter once again for the Silver Club in 1748.

The Rules of Play under which the first competition took place are still in existence and appear on the last two pages of the first Minute Book of the Honourable Company, signed by John Rattray. A copy is kept at Muirfield. The next oldest written Rules of Golf known to exist are the first Rules of the Royal and Ancient Club dated 1754. Both those, and the Regulations instituting the first Silver Cup competition of the Royal and Ancient Golf Club, are identical with those produced by the 'Gentlemen Golfers' – with a single exception to allow for the varying local conditions at the links at Leith and St. Andrews. The similarity between the two sets of rules is scarcely surprising since the 'Gentlemen Golfers' were represented at the first Competition of the Gentlemen of Fife, later to become the Royal and Ancient. A Minute of the former reads:

> Leith, 9 March 1754, Robert Douglas, writer in Edinburgh, having represented to the Captain and Gentlemen Golfers present that several Gentlemen of the County of Fife had contributed for a Silver Club to be played for annually upon the Links of St. Andrews and did in their name desire to know what day would be most convenient for the Gentlemen Golfers here to honour the Gentlemen of Fife with their presence on that occasion.

The Rules of Play of 'The Gentlemen Golfers' and the Royal and Ancient contain thirteen clauses. Within their small scope they contain all the root of the matter, and there will be many to claim that today's greatly extended clauses, and the numerous sub-clauses, have effected only minimal improvements. No doubt the Gentlemen Golfers' Rules were propagated in South Britain by the great Dr. Carlyle of Inveresk (commonly called Jupiter Carlyle) when he visited London accompanied by his friends, Dr. Robertson, the historian from Gladsmuir, and John Hume of Athelstaneford, author of the vilified *Douglas*. Dr. Carlyle recorded how, as they passed through Kensington on their way to play with David

Garrick, the Coldstream Regiment were changing guard and, on seeing their clubs, gave three cheers in honour of a diversion peculiar to Scotland.

Within a few years finance had become a problem for the Honourable Company. In 1758 the Records of the Edinburgh Golfers mention that a levy of five shillings sterling for maintenance was paid by twenty-nine members to Mr. James Cheape, the Club Treasurer; and in 1762 a Minute reads:

> The Captain and Council of the Edinburgh Golfers having taken under consideration the expense necessary attending the Drainage of the Links for the convenience of the said Gentlemen recommended to Mr Cheape, their Treasurer, to make up and give to the Captain and Council as soon as he conveniently can, a state of the funds in his hands as they have reason to believe there is not sufficient at present in his hands to answer the said expense. It is therefore resolved to open a subscription amongst the Golfers to make up any deficiency that may happen in consequence thereof.

Discipline also exercised the minds of the Captain and his Council as illustrated by two instances from the Minutes:

> Leith 4 August 1753.
> The Captain considering the negligence of the former Clerk and Agents of the Golfers does hereby with the assent of the Golfers depose them and for the future appoints Archibald Govan, Writer in Edinburgh, to be their Clerk, Agent and Procurator Fiscall.

and:

> The Captain and his Council considering that Mr. David Lyon ane Eminent Golfer, after subscribing and engaging himself to play for the Silver Club this day has not only not started for the Club But contrary to the Duty of his Allegiance has withdrawn himself from the Captain and his Company and has dined in another house after having bespoke a particular Dish for himself in Luckie Clephans. The Captain therefore with the advice of his Council appoints the procurator Fiscall to endyte the said David Lyon for the above offence . . . and hereby orders the Culprit to be cited to answer here on Saturday next.
>
> HENRY SETON,
> Captain.

The precise punishment is unknown, but the Minutes record:

> Mr Lyon was this day tryed for the above offence of breach of allegiance and punished according to his deserts.

As his name ceased to appear among the entrants for the Silver Club, it seems probable that he was asked to resign.

On the 11th January, 1764, the Lord Provost, Magistrates and Council of Edinburgh agreed that whereas when it was presented in 1744 the Silver Club was open to

> as many Noblemen or Gentlemen or other Golfers from any part of Great Britain or Ireland as shall book themselves Eight days before or upon any of the Lawfull days of the week preceding the day appointed by the Magistrates for the Annual Match, shall have the privilege of playing for the said Club,

these regulations were

> too broad, for by it, persons of bad fame or such as are not fitt company for Gentlemen, may play for and winn the Silver Club and if that should happen upon being declared Captain he must of course take the Chair and preside in all the Golf meetings which are purposely intended to be played for and won by Nobelmen and Gentlemen only.

In future, entry for the Silver Club was confined to members of the Company of Edinburgh Golfers. We do not know whether this change of policy was due to the bad behaviour of any particular individual or whether it was due to congestion on the links on Medal Day, or even to an excess of bonhomie at the close of play. But restriction there was to be.

The first Regulations governing the Company, drawn up by the Captain and ex-Captains on 25th February, 1764, ordained that:

1. Every person inclining to be admitted a Member of the Club must be proposed by a Member the Saturday before the Election.
2. Every Member admitted must be balloted for.
3. At Admission every Member must pay half a guinea.
4. Every Member must attend the Meeting when the Club is played for if he is in Edinburgh or Leith, or must give a proper excuse for his absence otherwise he forfeits his place in the Society.
5. Every Member must pay Five Shillings yearly for keeping of the Links in Good Order, and that before the Club is played for.

A further regulation was added on 22nd December, 1764, concerning the election of new members:

> No person admitted without ballot and none unless at least 6 members present whereof two thirds must agree in selection.

Perhaps it was their newly discovered sense of propriety that led the Company to show an unaccustomed interest in their spiritual welfare:

Leith, March 15, 1764.

The Captain and Council taking into their serious consideration the deplorable situation of the Company in wanting a godly and pious Chaplain, They did entreat the Reverend Doctor John Dun, Chaplain to the Right Honourable the Earl of Galloway, to accept the office of being Chaplain to the Golfers; which desire the said Doctor, out of his great regard for the Glory of God and the good of the souls of the said Company, was religiously pleased to comply with. Therefore the Company and Council Did and Do hereby nominate, present, and appoint the said Rev. Doctor John Dun to be their Chaplain accordingly. The said Reverend Doctor did accept of the Chaplaincy, and in token thereof said Grace after dinner.

It was about this time, too, or a couple of years later, that Smollet, in his novel *Humphry Clinker*, recalled seeing on Leith Links

one particular set of golfers, the youngest of whom was turned fourscore. They were all gentlemen of independent fortunes, who had amused themselves with this pastime for the best part of a century, without having ever felt the least alarm from sickness or disgust, and they never went to bed without each having the best part of a gallon of claret in his belly.

Eventually, the convivial gatherings at Luckie Clephan's, and at another tavern known as 'Straiton's', scarcely seemed to satisfy their aspirations and funds were raised to build the Company's own Golf House. The foundation stone was laid on 2nd July, 1768:

Leith, July 2, 1768.

This day Wm. St. Clair of Roslin, Esq., the undoubted representative of the Honourable and Heretable G. M. M. of Scotland, In presence of Alexander Keith, Esq., Captain of the Honourable Company of Goffers, and other worthy Members of the Goffing Company, all Masons, the G. M., now in his Grand Climax of Goffing, laid the Foundation of the Goffing House in the S.E. corner thereof, by Three Strokes with the Mallet.

ALEXR. KEITH, C.
WM. ST. CLAIR, G.M.M.

Among those present was one Alexander Duncan. On this occasion he was representing Royal Blackheath as their Captain. He had been Captain of the Royal and Ancient in 1756 and was to become Captain of the Honourable Company in the spring of 1781, a record which is probably unique, especially as in October 1781 he won the Silver Club at St. Andrews and became Captain again there.

The Honourable Company's regulations of the time contain the prudent prescription: 'Balls taken from the Landlord of the Golfhouse to be paid before going out to play'. The genial use made of the new premises can be seen from the sad fate of Lieutenant Dalrymple in 1776, and the vinous order promulgated in 1782:

> Leith, Nov. 16, 1776.
> This day Lieutenant James Dalrymple of the 43rd Regiment, being convicted of playing five different times at Golf without his uniform, was fined only in six Pints, having confirmed the heinousness of his crime.
>
> JA. CHEAP
>
> At his own request he was fined of Three Pints more.

> Golf House, Jan. 19, 1782.
> That Port and Punch shall be the ordinary Drink of the Society, unless upon these days when the Silver Club and Cups is played for. At those Meetings Claret or any other Liquor more agreeable will be permitted.
>
> ALEXR. DUNCAN, Captain.

There is an impressive, round quality about the last Minute. This was clearly a club populated by survivors from the heroic age. Dr. Johnson would have approved. It was not a place for half-pint men.

At this time the Company enjoyed the inspired advice provided by their famous Secretary and Treasurer, 'Singing Jamie Balfour', a man of unusual talents, administrative, athletic, musical and convivial. Dr. Andrew Duncan recalled that his musical talents and amiable temper could not fail to support the hilarity and harmony of every company in which he was present. His appearance is familiar to many thousands of golfers from reproductions of his portrait by Sir Henry Raeburn. The original was sold during the Club's financial crisis of 1832–36, but the print which is preserved at Muirfield bears an attachment in Raeburn's own hand:

> Edinburgh, 6 May 1793.   Received from James Balfour, Esq., the sum of Thirty Guineas for his own portrait done for the Society of Golfers, Henry Raeburn.

For thirty guineas the Company got a bargain, for it is one of the best portraits by Raeburn, who was a member. It shows the Secretary seated by a table with the Company's Minute books. North Berwick Law in the distance forms a background, and the whole conception is much more alive than Raeburn's normal statuesque poses. It is easy to believe the many

stories of Balfour's unusual stamina, whether it was a case of singing
'When I ha'e a saxpence under my thoom', as tradition says was his
occupation when the portrait was painted, or carousing round Edinburgh
to the loyal Jacobite strains of 'The King shall enjoy his ain again', or
racing more sober companions down the High Street to the nearest
tavern for yet another bottle of claret. One of his favourite haunts was
Jenny Ha's, opposite Queensberry House, where claret could be drawn
from the butt by the gentry on their way home from the formalities of
dinner parties. There Jamie could be found drinking a formidable
mixture known as 'cappie ale', that is, ale laced with brandy and drunk
from a wooden bowl.

His passing was celebrated with due solemnity. A general meeting of the
Club held on 14th November, 1795, 'in memory of their worthy Secretary' was attended by twenty-seven members, all dressed in Mourning
'agreeable to the advertisement', and led by the Lord Provost of Edinburgh. After the dinner, four toasts were proposed. After proposing the
health of the Company and dedicating his glass, the Captain invited the
Company to drink

> To the memory of our worthy and late departed friend, Mr. James
> Balfour, whose benevolent and cheerful disposition, and happy social
> powers, while they captivated all, particularly endeared him to his
> numerous friends.

Then came 'Comfort and consolation to the friends and relations of
Mr. James Balfour', and in logical, though perhaps optimistic, succession,
'May the offices in this society held by Mr. Balfour be agreeably supplied
and attended to with that accuracy and precision for which he was
generally distinguished'. During this solemnity, which was truly affecting,
a profound silence was observed. The Minutes record that the Captain
then 'proceeded to general toasts'. Worthy Jamie, your memory is carefully cherished.

Another portrait of the period is that by Sir George Chalmers of an
eminent Captain of the time, William St. Clair of Roslin, who presided
over the Company's affairs in 1761, 1766 and 1771, and who was also
Grand Master Mason of Scotland. Whether it be because of St. Clair's
melancholy, almond-shaped face, his blue Scots bonnet, his scarlet tunic,
or his unbelievable method of addressing the ball, this is one of the most
famous of all golfing portraits. Sir Walter Scott described him as being
thin-flanked and broad-shouldered, built it would seem for the business

of war or the chase, a noble eye of chastened pride and undoubted authority. As a schoolboy, Scott had crowded with other Edinburgh boys to see him perform feats of strength at golf and archery. His portrait epitomises the elegant, mildly disdainful, approach associated with the Company of Golfers. Sad to say, this portrait, too, was sold during the Company's financial crisis, but it has found a worthy home with the Royal Company of Archers, and an excellent copy hangs above the fireplace in the Smoking Room at Muirfield. St. Clair died in 1778 and is buried among his ancestors in Roslin Chapel.

The year 1800 was an eventful one for the Honourable Company. In March the Magistrates or Edinburgh, in response to a petition, granted the Gentlemen Golfers a 'Seal of Cause', the effect being that, under the title 'The Honourable The Edinburgh Company of Golfers', the Club became a legal society or Body Corporate with full power to manage its own affairs. To date, the Honourable Company were under obligation to the Town Council to preserve at their own expense the links at Leith of which they were the lessees. In return for payment of an annual Feu Duty, they also had the feu of a piece of adjacent land upon which they had, at much expense, erected the Golf House. But, since they were not a Body Corporate, they had to hold the property in the name of a Trustee outwith the Club.

An abiding feature of life with the Honourable Company has always been the Dinner Matches; that is to say, matches made at Club Dinners for a named stake and between players sufficiently equal in skill as to encourage other members to wager on the outcome. The Bett Book records the matches since 1776. A fuller account of the idiosyncrasies of betting at Muirfield and the Dinner Matches is given later in the 'Wagers and Gambols' chapter. Until the end of the eighteenth century, there is hardly a mention of Dinner Matches being played anywhere but at Leith, although from early in the new century matches were played more and more at Musselburgh. When the Company first started playing for the Silver Club at Leith in 1774, the Links consisted of five holes – typical golfing country separated from the sea on the north by sand dunes. A General Meeting of the Club on 22nd April, 1775, resolved that:

In playing you are to strike off from the Braehead Hill and play to the Sawmill for the first hole. From the Sawmill to the North mid-hole for the second. To the East hole for the third; to the South mid-hole for the fourth and to the Thorntree hole for the fifth where the first round ends and every round (thence) to begin at the Thorntree hole, playing from that to the Sawmill as above until you come again to the Thorntree hole where every round ends.

The Club Golf Medal used to be played over two rounds of five holes each, the best recorded score for the ten holes being by Mr. H. M. Low in 1826 with 60 strokes.

The holes were all about 400 yards long and, in 1783, the bogey for the course seems to have been 35 strokes. But Leith Links was wet and drainage always a problem. During the Napoleonic Wars, too, military activities on the links became a repeated nuisance, and there were various other encroachments by cattle and by the general public which did not commend themselves to the Honourable Company intent on serious business. The members were gradually moving to Musselburgh for their exercise. This was inevitable, but the Council of the Club, who still recognised some debt to the City, were unwilling to accept the need for a move. In 1811, the Magistrates had presented a second Silver Club, since the first had no room on it for further balls to be attached. Indeed, the Council remained loyal to Leith, their original home, until increasing difficulties, combined with mismanagement, led to the financial situation which culminated in the forced sale of the Golf House, together with its contents, and the suspension of the Club Dinners.

This crisis has led to a belief long held that these events marked the decease of the Honourable Company, and that it was only resuscitated some years later at Musselburgh. This misconception probably derives from a statement in *Golf, a Royal and Ancient Game*, by Robert Clark, published in 1875, which reappears in *The Golf Book of East Lothian*, by the Rev. John Kerr (1896). The former writes:

> In 1831 some alterations having been made in the Links and the green ceasing to be attractive, it was advisable to dispose of the Golf House. For an interval of five years 1831–1836 the Company was defunct.

He lamented the selling of the property within the Golf House as 'a very foolish thing' as 'many articles which to the Company would now have been of priceless value were dispersed never to be seen again'. The Minutes for the period have not been found but, shortly before the 1939–45 War, an exhaustive search of public registers, City records, newspapers and other sources of possible information was made. A number of documents of different dates and importance was discovered at Muirfield, and it is now possible to see more clearly what happened in this unhappy period.

Since 1764 there had been no annual subscription, apart from the 5s. for maintenance of the links for the Silver Club competition, and entry money of half a guinea. Since this was not enough to meet expenses, the Golf House was mortgaged in 1824 to secure an advance of £500. In 1828 Mr. Henry M. Low, lately Captain and a Writer to the Signet in Edinburgh, arranged a second mortgage of £200. In 1829 Low was appointed Secretary, and in February 1830 he fled the country, hopelessly indebted to his clients and others. (This makes it easier to understand why the last entry in the Minute Book of the period is merely a record of the 1830 Silver Club Competition.)

The financial position was steadily deteriorating. With no annual subscription, few new members, and most of the playing taking place at Musselburgh, little money was coming into the Golf House at Leith. At the end of 1831 the mortgage interest was in arrears and on 30th January, 1832, Andrew Clason, the agent for the Bondholders and a member of the Council of the Honourable Company, was in communication with the Treasurer, and a General Meeting, held on 18th May, 1832, appointed Mr. John Kennedy as agent to examine the affairs of the Club and report. In order to appease the creditors, it was found necessary to dispose of the moveable assets. The furniture and furnishings of the Golf House and the portraits were accordingly sold on 29th August, 1833, and realised the sum of £106. 9s. 10d. It would appear that there were only five portraits, including those of William St. Clair and James Balfour, and the furnishings for a dining-room.

There was fortunately no question of the Club trophies being sold. In spite of the distressed circumstances from which the Club was trying to extricate itself, loyalty to Leith continued, and on 18th September, 1833, the lease of the links was extended until Martinmas 1834 – in itself evidence that the Club was far from defunct. Repayment of the first mortgage of £500 was now being demanded. To meet this, the principal asset remaining had to be realised and, on 19th January, 1834, by order of the Bondholders, the Golf House was sold and realised £1,130.

The Honourable Company were not yet clear of their financial troubles since the most complicated law actions and counteractions arose out of the mortgage for £200 arranged by the fleeing Secretary, and it was not until 11th November, 1835, that £260. 18s. 8d. was deposited in the Royal Bank of Scotland 'for behoof of the Honourable Company of Edinburgh Golfers', and not until 25th July, 1836, that a figure could be named which would be available for the use of the Club.

As the Dinners had never been self-supporting, and as there was still no annual subscription, it was not possible to hold them until the financial tangle was unravelled. When this had been achieved, a General Meeting was held in Edinburgh on 26th July, 1836, when it was decided to continue the Dinners at Musselburgh. The last tie with Leith was severed.

CHAPTER II

THE THIRTEEN ARTICLES

Compliance with the laws of the game is essential so that justice may be done and the defeated player should not nourish a grievance that he has been outwitted by some form of gamesmanship or other chicanery. Invoking the letter of the law is, however, a different thing. It was a practice deprecated by the early Gentlemen Golfers, who relied for guidance on a very rudimentary set of rules, and, since then, by true golfers everywhere.

The Honourable Company are on record as being concerned with the first golfing legislation, and it is on their earliest rules of 1744 that all subsequent codes have been based. But this seems to have been an accident of history. The Gentlemen Golfers, as they were then called, were the first organised society and, on this account, could reasonably be expected to produce the original rules, which fortunately have been preserved. Although the members discharged this first responsibility, they did not manifest any great zeal in keeping the laws up to date nor, beyond minor alterations, did they refine them to meet changing conditions. The 1744 code, embodied practically word for word by the Royal and Ancient Club when they drew up their own original rules in 1754, was revised in 1775, and again in 1809. These three sets form an important element in the history of the game and, taken together, they are the Honourable Company's contribution to the laws of golf. Long before the Royal and Ancient appointed a committee of fifteen of its members in 1897 to be the Rules of Golf Committee (with terms of reference that have remained unaltered), the Honourable Company had gracefully abrogated any residual authority to make laws or to give authoritative interpretations on contentious cases. Not many members would endorse the Rev. John Kerr's rueful comment on the gradual transfer of power to the Royal and Ancient: 'Proud as we are of the history and tradition of the Honourable Company, we must ever regard it in the light of a disinherited heir to the title and estates now enjoyed by the great club which, on the opposite

JAMIE BALFOUR
Secretary and Treasurer till 1795

shore of the Forth, is a law to all others.' The Honourable Company have never lacked strong personalities capable of impressing their opinions and attitudes on their fellow-members, but it is perhaps not wholly fortuitous that none of them ever sought to earn a reputation as a law-maker or a golf jurist. Sea-lawyers seem to have had no welcome at the port of Leith.

The 1744 code contained thirteen rules, and the revised 1809 version contained only one more. They set out the main conditions under which the game was to be played – conditions which have shown remarkably little variation since then. They say where and how the ball is to be teed; the ball is not to be changed during a hole; stones or other temporary obstructions can only be removed if lying within a club's length: provision is made for the unplayable ball, and for moving one of the balls if they lie touching each other: the line to the hole is not to be marked and there is to be no deliberate play on the opponent's ball. The nature of the stroke is also defined, although only by implication. Taken together, the 1744 code offered a good framework which has stood the test of time.

It would, however, be wrong to suggest that the present-day rules could ever be reduced to anything approaching the brevity of the early regulations, or that the jurisprudence of the learned members of the Rules of Golf Committee is otiose. Inevitably, the rules have had to be modified to cope with the vast growth in the number of players and the extension of the game to more exotic conditions and diverse countries. The omissions from the Honourable Company's first code also give some clue to the purpose of the original rules and the circumstances in which they were drawn up.

The 1744 rules prescribe no penalties for malefactors. There is no mention of what was to be done to anyone who changed his ball during the playing of the hole or who marked out the line on the ground with his club. The explanation can scarcely be that the original Gentlemen Golfers were so much more law-abiding than their successors. Much more likely, the succinct form of the early rules arose from the fact that, in their original conception, they were intimate regulations drawn up to govern the competitions on Leith Links for the Silver Club. The competitors were few in number; their proclivities were known to each other; offences could easily be detected; and the members of the Honourable Company could be left to deal with (it is to be hoped, exceptional) offenders according to their demerits. The significance of the earlier rules is, therefore, historical, because of their very antiquity, and domestic, in reflecting the

C

practice on Leith Links. From a fairly early stage there appears to have been variation on other links. The Royal Burgess Golfing Society, for example, allowed a striker to play on his opponent's ball and, at St. Andrews, a ball lying in water had to be picked out and dropped, under penalty of a stroke. At Leith, teeing up was permitted in the same circumstances.

The thirteen articles of the Gentlemen Golfers are no encyclopaedia of golf's common or case law, but they are worth a brief scrutiny *seriatim* to elicit the spirit and intention of the first lawmakers.

I '*You must tee your ball within one club's length of the hole.*'

This provides an instant reminder that play on the earliest links was continuous, from hole to hole. A separate teeing ground is not mentioned in any golf rules before 1875. Judged from early prints, showing spectators crowding round the protagonists on the edge of the hole, putting must have been hazardous by itself, apart from the difficulty of finding an agreeable spot 'within one club's length of the hole' on which to tee the ball. This primitive practice continued for some time, the maximum distance from the hole being extended to four clubs' lengths in 1777 and to eight in 1828. The teeing ground proper did not get its first definition until 1893. The Honourable Company still adhere to the old practice of indicating the tee by two simple marks (large white balls) at right angles to the line of play. The holes are neither named – a practice which has for long been falling into general desuetude – nor numbered, and lengths are not shown. This unhelpful lack of information has often been criticised, but no changes ever seem to have been contemplated. Obstinate conservatism, or a subconscious wish to adhere to primal simplicity? It is not for me to say.

II '*Your tee must be upon the ground.*'

At first sight, this seems a curious rule. Where else could the tee be but on the ground? Even the doggerel rhymster, Thomas Mathison, in his dreadful 'heroi-comical poem in three cantos', called 'The Goff' (1743), confirms that this was the usual custom:

> Lo, tatter'd Irus, who their armour bears,
> Upon the green two little pyr'mids rears,
> On these they place two balls with careful eye,
> That with Clarinda's breasts for colour vye.

But there must have been some necessity for the stern injunction of Article II, since the Royal Burgess Society later (1776) enacted it in even more peremptory terms: 'Your tee must be on the ground and unconnected with any conductor or leader to the ball.' The only sportsman known to have challenged this basic ordinance was that sprightly surgeon, Sir Harold Gillies, in the 1930s, who, Maskelynewise, teed his ball on the top of a piece of indiarubber tubing superimposed on a beer bottle. It was not long before it became apparent that the Royal and Ancient were not amused.

III *'You are not to change the ball you strike off the tee.'*

The advantage which could have been gained by putting down a new feather ball was so great that this was an essential requirement. The feathery, with an outer covering of sewn leather, can seldom have been perfectly round: this would soon show itself after a couple of strokes, especially with the crude weapons and on pitted fairways of the earlier days, and a player under pressure would soon long to replace his now misshapen ball with a new Gourlay. There is, surprisingly, nothing in the thirteen articles about what happened to the unwary competitors who played the wrong ball. This may well have been a case for reference to the Captain. Under a separate provision (Regulation IX of the Act of Council and Regulation to be observed by those who played yearly for the City of Edinburgh's Silver Club), 'All disputes touching the Golf, amongst Golfers shall be determined by the Captain and any two or three of the Subscribers he shall call to his assistance.'

IV *'You are not to remove Stones, Bones or any Break Club, for the sake of playing your Ball, except upon the Fair Green and that only within a Club's length of your Ball.'*

The reference to bones recalls the still rural nature of Leith Links which were used, to the discomfiture of the Gentlemen Golfers, for grazing cattle. The word 'break club' remained in the rule until 1888, although comparatively few golfers could then have recognised one. The general sense of the article has, however, remained with temporary variation, and 'within a club's length' remains the general practice, except in hazards. The term 'Fair Green' is used for the putting green. The first reference to the putting green is in the 1812 rules of the Royal and Ancient. The 1744 Rules of the Honourable Company give no indication of the use of the putting green in early days. But in their rules of 1839 it was 'considered not to exceed twenty yards from the hole', which was the modern definition until recently when it became 'all the ground of the hole being played which is specially prepared for putting or otherwise defined as such by the Committee'.

V   'If your Ball come among watter or any wattery filth, you are at liberty to take out your Ball and bringing it behind the hazard and teeing it, you may play it with any club and allow your Adversary a Stroke, for so getting out your ball.'

Lift out of water and play from behind under penalty of a stroke has, for all practicable purposes, been the general rule ever since 1744 – as those who have sadly recovered their balls from the Swilcan, the Barry Burn and other less celebrated rivulets will know – but the explicit concession in this article that the ball could be teed was probably a local rule. Much of the turf at Leith was known to be soft and spongy and the prospect of recovery from the 'wattery filth' being followed by a plugged drop may have been thought too likely to induce apoplexy, outwith the range of recourse to Lucky Clephan's for an appropriate cordial.

VI   'If your balls be found anywhere touching one another you are to lift the first ball, till you play the last.'

The necessity for this article also evokes the circumstances in which the original rules were framed. The feathery ball, which had no resilience to speak of, would be much more likely to nestle against another one than would the later gutty or Haskell. Contiguity may therefore have been a more recurring problem in 1744 than it could conceivably be nowadays. The rule was needed to prevent acute, physical aggression. In 1775 the definition of 'touching' was extended to six inches – which later became the minimum distance between balls in a stymie.

VII   'At Holing, you are to play your Ball honestly for the Hole, and not play upon your Adversary's Ball, not lying in your way to the Hole.'

The peculiar interest in this article, which is also germane to the preceding one, is that, from an early stage, it was necessary to prevent ardent competitors yielding to the temptation to have a smack at the enemy's ball. It is evident that the legislators of the Honourable Company were opposed to this croquet-like behaviour and did not look with favour on a crafty golfer who took pains to play a glancing shot which drove his opponent's ball into some 'wattery filth'. The Royal and Ancient endorsed this approach, but the Royal Burgess Club, not without controversy, continued to allow an unrestricted right to play on the opposing ball for nearly another century – until 1838. The proposition that this was originally, and still is, a natural impulse on the part of golfers is perhaps supported by the continued existence of penalties, both in match and stroke play, for disturbing the opposing ball. In 1784, however, the sophistication, and sophistry, of the stymie still lay a little ahead.

VIII   *'If you should lose your Ball, by its being taken up, or any other way you are to go back to the Spot, where you struck last, and drop another Ball, and allow your adversary a Stroke for the misfortune.'*

The penal consequence of losing your ball has varied, for no very logical reason, in a strangely cyclical manner. The Honourable Company's original penalty of stroke and distance lasted till 1868. From then until 1920 the rule was even simpler, namely, lost ball, lost hole. Since then there has been, in turn, stroke and distance, distance only, and, latterly, the original provision repeated. This also seems to have been a matter where there was more than usual divergence between individual clubs. As early as 1776, for example, the Royal Burgess were enacting lost ball, lost hole; and at St. Andrews, too, there were changes of heart. But at Leith there were good reasons for thinking that loss of hole was too severe a penalty. Playing, as they did, on public links, open to interference by non-golfers, the Honourable Company found that 'There was a very real peril often awaiting a new ball lying out of the sight of its owner'. Such depredations were severe enough in themselves without losing the hole as well.

IX   *'No man at Holing his Ball is to be allowed, to mark his way to the Hole with his Club or anything else.'*

This was another rule which identified a basic temptation. It was explicitly re-enacted in the Rules of the Royal Burgess of 1776, Royal Aberdeen 1783, by the Honourable Company again in 1809, and by the Royal and Ancient in 1812. The concentration of legal authority is evidence that the offending practice was always liable to be adopted by the less meticulous, and was regarded with particular disfavour. At Aberdeen it was forbidden 'to draw a line', and the player's partner was not allowed to stand at the hole 'nor direct him in aiming'. At St. Andrews, players were vigorously prohibited from placing 'any mark to direct you to the Hole'. Smoother greens and well-groomed fairways have now made this proscription less essential, but a caddy pointing the way to the hole is still forbidden to touch the surface of the putting green.

X '*If a Ball be stopp'd by any person, Horse, Dog or anything else, the Ball so stopp'd must be play'd where it lyes.*'

This is another article which illustrates the deplorably congested conditions at Leith under which the Gentlemen Golfers played. Dogs still interfere with play, although very infrequently are they struck by balls, as the article contemplates, but the neighing of horses seldom distracts the player's concentration today. The Honourable Company's 1775 Rules re-enacted the provision in a significantly different form: 'If a ball be stopped by accident, it must be played where it lies, but, if stopped by the adversary, his Cady or servant, the party who stops the ball to lose one'. This sinister change immediately suggests that some unscrupulous player had been known to engage an assistant to interfere with the free progress of the enemy's ball. The article is, however, a simple one compared with the great volume of detailed rules which is now found necessary to solve such problems as 'moving ball stopped', 'ball lodged in anything moving', or 'ball at rest displaced by outside agency'. Case law to deal with these unpredictable circumstances has multiplied over the years, and the original article would not now be thought adequate to deal with such bizarre incidents as Harry Bradshaw's ball coming to rest in a bottle at the decisive stage of the Open Championship at Sandwich in 1949. Or would it?

XI '*If you draw your Club, in order to Strike and proceed so far in the Stroke, as to be bringing down your Club: If then your Club shall break, in any way, it is to be Accounted a Stroke.*'

This article, which defines the 'stroke' by implication, was perhaps the most metaphysical of the Honourable Company's rules. It corresponds to the modern definition of a stroke as being 'the forward movement of the Club made with the intention of fairly striking and moving the ball'. The original was a well drafted regulation. It is easy to visualise William St. Clair, who must have used an exceptionally supple-shafted club if he really played, as his portrait shows, with an exaggeratedly closed stance, cracking an indifferent shaft at the top of his swing and being accounted to have played. The article also foreshadows that recurring disease known as the 'staggers' which afflicts even the most experienced players and leaves them paralysed at the top of their swing, totally unable to complete the stroke.

XII '*He whose Ball lyes farthest from the Hole is obliged to play first.*'

The need for a specific provision on what is really a point of etiquette is not easy to understand. It is scarcely to be supposed that the competitors on Leith Links were so intemperate, incautious or ill-mannered that they advanced on the hole playing a quick succession of shots without regard to what their opponents were doing. The necessity for this article is all the more surprising since, as H. H. Gardiner-Hill in his penetrating analysis of the early rules (*History of Golf in Britain*, (1952)) comments, the Honourable Company did not, curiously, make any mention in their code of the primary point that the ball must be played wherever it lies. Presumably, this principle was so well known that no rule was needed, although it might have been expected to give rise to more dispute than the order of play. Rule 6 of the 1775 code did, however, enact that 'in no case except what is mentioned can a Ball be lifted, but must be played where it lyes'.

XIII '*Neither Trench, Ditch or Dyke, made for the presentation of the Links, nor the Scholar's Holes or the Soldier's Lines, Shall be accounted a Hazard. But the Ball is to be taken out and Tee'd and play'd with any Iron Club.*'

This was clearly a local rule, justified by the soggy conditions at Leith. From time to time, the Honourable Company's records emphasise that Leith was a wet course. In 1778, £28 was spent on draining parts of the green and over £60 was spent on the same purpose in 1802–03. But it was not only the dampness of the terrain that caused anxiety. The drilling of the local Territorials, the Mid Lothian Volunteers, and other Cavalry stationed in the vicinity, was not compatible with a good lie on the 'fair green', and was, without doubt, one of the factors that led to the eventual move to Musselburgh. The reference to the 'Soldier's Lines' is also of interest because the incautious draftsman, who absorbed the Honourable Company's 1744 code in the rules of the Royal and Ancient ten years later, reproduced the military reference although, unlike the 'Scholar's Holes', it had no meaning at St. Andrews. A final oddity about this rule is the reference to playing without penalty only with an iron club. The distinction between playing with a wooden, or 'timber' club and an iron one is incomprehensible in modern conditions.

The thirteen articles are brief and understandable, and, though golfing conditions have changed, they still have very considerable force. No draftsman could ask for more after the passage of more than two centuries. John Rattray, Captain, when he signed them cannot have realised that he had acquired a more certain passport to immortality than many of his successors in office.

The first amendment to the original articles was recorded in 1758 when Thomas Boswall, Captain, decreed that 'The 5th and 13th Articles of the foregoing Laws having occasioned frequent Disputes, it is found convenient That in all time Coming the Law shall be That in no case whatever a Ball shall be Lifted without a Stroke except it is in the Scholar's holes, when it may be taken and teed and played with any Iron Club without losing a stroke and in all other Cases The Ball must be played where it lyes Except it is at least half covered with Water or Filth When it may if the Player chooses be taken out Teed and played with any Club upon Loosing a Stroke.' This was required to remove an apparent contradiction in the earlier code. Under the original fifth article, when a ball was found in water or filth, it could be teed and played with any club, but with the loss of a stroke. This rule was at variance with that contained in Article XIII which allowed a ball found in any of the various circumstances described (and the ditches or dykes mentioned must have been water-logged) to be teed and played with an iron club – but without penalty. The freedom from penalty was accordingly restricted to the Scholar's Holes which must have been considered a particularly unfair hazard.

Next came one further refinement – dealing with the same topic – in 1771. It was resolved that 'when a Golf Ball lyes half Ball in water, in the Green, the player shall be at liberty to take out the Ball And cause his Cadie drop the Ball behind the hazard, he may either play with the Iron without losing a Stroke or he may Tee his Ball and play with a Timber club and lose a Stroke'. That eminent authority on early rules, and the rules of the Honourable Company in particular, C. B. Clapcott, in his 1939 monograph observed the oddity that it was the 'Cadie' who was required to drop the ball. 'That the player should not have been obliged to soil his hands unnecessarily can be understood. But could he not have been given the option? Or was the "Cadie" more likely to drop fairly than the player?'

A further revision in 1775 produced only five differences from the original 1744 code, and those mainly in degree, namely –

(1) The teeing ground was removed further from the hole.
(2) On the green, stones and loose impedimenta might now be re-moved at a greater distance than a club's length from the ball.
(3) The penalty for a lost ball was reduced to stroke only.
(4) A ball within six inches of another one could be lifted.
(5) A penalty of a stroke was imposed if the adversary or his caddie stopped the ball.

The 1809 code – and then we may soon leave the Honourable Company's rule-making activities – contained further variations, some of them ob-viously related to the local conditions at Leith. For example, the soft condition of the ground, and the likelihood of the ball becoming plugged, made it necessary to agree that 'if a ball stick fast in the ground it may be loosend', and a ball which lay 'in any of the water-trades on the green' could be lifted and dropped without penalty. Any disputes respecting the play were to be determined by the Captain 'or senior counsellor' present. A revised version in 1839 has a more modern look about it, and a brisk codicil which has a familiar ring – 'All Spectators at Golf Matches are requested to be silent, and to stand still, while the Parties are striking or about to strike.' But we are now well on the way to universal acceptance of the rules promulgated by the Royal and Ancient, although these were not given formal authority till just before the turn of the century.

The Honourable Company's early rules were framed with match play in mind, and some of them make no sense in terms of stroke play. That was in keeping with the temper of the times.

It is a pertinent question, by way of concluding this chapter, to enquire what is the interest or relevance today of these early articles. Are they a matter of concern only to the professional golf historian, or to that meticulous golfer who has a copy of the latest rules always available for immediate reference? There is more to it than that. The photostat copy of the first articles that hangs in the Smoking Room at Muirfield, the portrait of William St. Clair, and the anonymous white balls that mark the teeing ground are all of a piece. Today's successors to the Gentlemen Golfers would at least like to think that they were still playing their ball 'honestly for the hole'.

CHAPTER III

THE ANCHOR AND MUSSEL

For fifty years after leaving Leith, the Honourable Company made their home at Musselburgh. In retrospect it seems as though this was almost consciously a period of marking time. The Company arrived at the 'Honest Toun' with some vestigial prestige, derived from their antiquity, which was sufficient to allow them to retain a name and an organisation. But active members were few and the strength of the cadre that transferred from Leith Links was built up only gradually.

In the course of this half century the main changes in the golfing scene were the arrival of the 'gutty' ball and, partly in consequence, the enormous spread of the popularity of the game. Speaking at a dinner given by the London Scottish Golf Club in the 1890s, Lord Wemyss (Captain of Luffness) attributed the rise in the number of golfers to three causes, namely, the spread of education (sic), the invention of the gutta-percha ball, and the publicised activities of Mr. A. J. Balfour.

The 'gutty' was certainly revolutionary. The name was derived from the Malayan 'gueta', a gum, and 'pertcha', a cloth. There are conflicting accounts of who first thought of making golf balls out of the newly imported gum, but it was Mr. H. T. Peters who claimed that he had played the first round with one in Scotland – at Innerleven in 1848. Its arrival was appropriately celebrated by the amateur versifier, Dr. William Graham:

> Hail! Gutta Percha, precious gum!
> O'er Scotland's links lang may ye bum.
> Some purse-proud billies haw and hum,
> And say ye'er douf at fleein';
> But let them try ye fairly out
> Wi' ony balls for days about,
> Your merits they will loudly tout,
> And own they hae been leein'.

According to the Rev. John Kerr, Peters and his brother used to play with gutties with a piece of lead fixed in the centre to make them putt more accurately. (A well struck putt must have made a fine resonant sound.) At all events, the number of golfers rose proportionately with the manufacture of gutties. Cheaper, more durable, and more available than the old feather ball, it remained unchallenged until the invention of the Haskell in 1902. The gutty was much more manageable than the feather, especially when it was accidentally discovered that the tendency to 'duck' could be cured by giving the ball a notched, abrasive marking. Initially the favourite gutties were made by the leading club makers from St. Andrews, including Tom Morris and Robert Forgan. Others had such exotic names as the O.K., the Ocobo, the Clan and the Agrippa – the last being the favourite of two great Muirfield figures, J. E. Laidlay and Leslie Balfour-Melville.

A. J. Balfour was the first of a long line of Prime Ministers who have testified to the game's relaxing powers. He was eventually a member of the Honourable Company, but it is as a North Berwick man, playing on the links there, protected by detectives during the Irish troubles, that he is chiefly remembered, and it was there that he took part in a famous recurring foursome with J. E. Laidlay against John Penn, M.P., and W. M. de Zoete. Over the whole period when they played, Balfour and Laidlay were said to be 'a few holes to the good'. Many years later, Bernard Darwin, in recollection, endorsed the view that A. J.'s affection for the game was extremely important in its development. The popular weekly, *Answers*, ingenuously reported in April 1894 that:

> Croquet is fast becoming popular again, but it can never take the place of golf, which is one of the most fashionable games of the day. The Right Hon. A. J. Balfour, M.P., is a really clever golfer; and he possesses a remarkably fine set of *silver-mounted caddies*, which were presented to him by one of his Scottish admirers.

The mummification of caddies has never really been an indigenous pastime in East Lothian. But we are anticipating.

The Honourable Company's decision to move had been a gradual one, and as early as 1828 – abandoning the memory of Lucky Clephan's for the prospect of the Anchor and Mussel – the Club resolved to dine at Musselburgh and to invite the Magistrates and Town Council. At the decisive meeting in July 1836, held at Barry's Hotel, 'the members present unanimously elected Mr. William Wood to be captain for the year, and resolved in the meantime to meet at Musselburgh, within M'Kendrick's Inn, on the first Saturday of each of the three ensuing months'. Mr. Wood responded to his election by winning the Club medal in the following year. At the same time, another Mr. Wood – John – was punished by a fine of 'two tappit hens (a quart measure) for appearing on the Links without a red coat'.

There is a nostalgic belief, widely held, that at one time golf links were entirely populated by picturesque figures resplendently turned out in scarlet coats. Distance lends enchantment, as Wooster would say, but, alas, this is not really so. It is true that in 1787 Lord Elcho, as Captain, had signed a Minute approving a Club uniform and appointing John Paterson, Tailor in Edinburgh, as Tailor for the Society.

At almost the same time (1780) the Royal and Ancient took into consideration that their golfing jackets were in bad condition and that they needed new ones which were to be of red with yellow buttons. Four years later they settled for a uniform coat, a grander garment, consisting of a dark blue velvet cape with white buttons and an embroidered club and ball of silver on each side of the cape. By 1820, however, the aspirations of the Royal and Ancient were satisfied with a plain blue coat and the Society button.

The Honourable Company appear to have become disgracefully indifferent to standards of turnout and, at their Annual General Meeting on 3rd April, 1888, it was declared 'That the terms of a minute of the Club dated 1787, recognising a Club Uniform, be ratified and re-enacted, viz. – That the Club Uniform be a scarlet coat with blue cloth collar and club buttons, and a blue cloth cap. That it be compulsory for the Captain to appear at the dinners in a Uniform coat, but that it be voluntary on the part of other members. That there be no prescribed shape of coat either for golfing or dining.' The Captain and ex-Captains still wear their scarlet coats at Match Dinners. This practice ensures at least an appearance of decorum at the top table; but for rank and file members the red uniform has long been in abeyance. It is very doubtful if it was ever universally, or anything like universally, worn. Bernard Darwin, from his deep lore of golfing knowledge, could find little to support the ubiquitous red coat theory, but he did recall that, in his youth, undergraduates at Cambridge affected scarlet tunics with light blue collars adorned with the university arms in gold and ermine on the pocket. Oxford had similar jackets with dark blue. But soon both Universities discarded their more colourful clothes for ordinary gray, and another elegant form of dress had disappeared.

Mr. Stair Gillon, in his admirable account of the Company's activities from 1891 to 1914, printed privately in 1946, records that by the time the Honourable Company left Musselburgh 'nobody dressed up for golf'. Trousers were more common than knickerbockers. The stiff-collared, tweed-coated, gentlemen's attire worn on the course varied from that worn in Princes Street, Edinburgh, only in coverings for head and feet. The cloth caps, often with green-lined peaks, outnumbered the deer-stalkers. Massive nailed boots were worn, sometimes with spats. But red coats were a rarity and 'Favourite, frayed, special coats may have been there; but they did not catch the eye in the dining-room, and on the links the eye was on the ball, or just off it, or on the line, or scouring the rough'. But the myth that all ancestral golfers were dressed in red has died hard.

Shortly after the move to Musselburgh in 1836, the rules governing the award of the Silver Club were changed. In future the winner of the Club's competition received a Gold Medal and the Silver Club became the official symbol of office of the Captain who was no longer elected solely for his prowess on the Links. This widened the field of election to include genial sportsmen who could not compete with the Corinthians, but the Captain still has to attach a silver ball to mark his term of office.

At first the Club had no premises of their own, part of the Grandstand of the Racecourse being used, and this by itself gave rise to a feeling of impermanence. The Course was shared with the Royal Musselburgh Golf Club and any members of the general public who might care to play golf on it. There was still no annual subscription. As expenses were small, this seemed of no consequence, but it is curious that a question of principle seems to have been involved since, on 7th December, 1838, thirty-five members of the Honourable Company, who were also members of the Royal and Ancient, wrote to the Committee of the latter Club protesting against their proposal 'requiring an Annual Subscription of one guinea'. In their opinion 'It has been invariably found that an annual subscription to a Club for sheer amusement has prevented that Club from "thriving".' In view of the financial difficulties which had all but extinguished the Honourable Company only a few years previously, this seems a remarkably myopic observation from a society in which the learned professions were heavily represented. It is also odd that the letter should have been included in the Minutes of the Honourable Company. It may have been inserted as an article of faith. It also shows the link still existing between the Honourable Company and the Royal and Ancient.

As the membership increased, so the Honourable Company undertook a larger share of the responsibility for the upkeep of the course. The Club had begun at Musselburgh with a credit balance of £202. 5s. 3d. and up to 1857 the principal item of expenditure in the accounts was the amount spent on wines. This was usually champagne at 75s. to 80s. per dozen.

In 1840, T. Alexander, one of a long line of famous ball-makers from Musselburgh, received £4. 4s. as 'Club Officer'. In 1850, the indefatigable John Gourlay, from the famous family of club makers, received £10 'for making the new course', and afterwards an annual fee of £5 for his attention to the interests of the Club. Gourlay had an unrivalled reputation as a feather ball-maker. A Gourlay ball was described as 'white as snow, hard as lead and elastic as a whalebone' or 'a Gourley pill, the best o' a' '. He was also the tenant of the Grandstand and, as such, supervised the races. He appears from all contemporary accounts to have been a man of natural authority. His proficiency at the game, his skill in making balls, and his impartial decisions on the rules of the game, made him one of the Honourable Company's best-known servants. On his death, in 1869, play was suspended until after his funeral, and over two hundred golfers attended the last ceremony at Inveresk.

In 1865 the Company, finding that the Grandstand was not satisfactory for refreshment and relaxation, built a Clubhouse at the west end of the Links. For this purpose the Golf House Club was formed and it was arranged that 'Any present member of the Honourable Company of Edinburgh Golfers may become a member and any person who shall thereafter be admitted a member shall also become a member of the Golf House Club'. In 1871 all new members paid an entrance fee of £2. 2s. to the Honourable Company and £3. 3s. to the Golf House Club, together with an annual subscription of £1. 1s. to the latter. Despite their pious protestations to the Royal and Ancient, the members of the Honourable Company were gradually becoming conscious of the need for an assured subscription income. The Clubhouse, which was ready for use by 1868, cost about £2,115 and, towards this, the Honourable Company lent £480 without interest, the rest being borrowed from the Bank.

Throughout their stay at Musselburgh the Honourable Company, possibly able to call on expert legal advice from their members, actively resisted any interference with the right of playing golf on the Links. In

1852 they joined with a Dr. Sanderson in preventing the Town authorities from fencing the Links, and in 1889 they stopped a road being made across the course. With the arrival of the Royal Burgess and Bruntsfield Links Clubs at Musselburgh, there were four Clubs owning Clubhouses and making the Green their home course, and it was perhaps inevitable that each should eventually find a permanent home elsewhere. In 1877, at the suggestion of the Honourable Company, the management of the Links was entrusted to a Joint Committee composed of representatives from the four Clubs. The annual contribution for upkeep was fixed on a capitation basis according to the membership of each Club. Towards the end of their stay, the Honourable Company were apparently paying 2s. 6d. per head on a membership of 400. After the move to Muirfield this was reduced to a payment to cover membership of 200, and even this ceased on the sale of the Clubhouse in 1893.

On 22nd May, 1879, it was noted that the two Silver Clubs presented by the City of Edinburgh were quite filled with silver balls affixed by the several Captains from 1744 to 1867, but that, since the latter date, no Captain had added a ball, as was customary. This delinquency had to be corrected, and the Secretary was instructed to get an estimate from Hamilton & Inches, the Edinburgh jewellers, for a new silver club and balls 'and thereafter to write the several Captains since 1867 for their authority to order silver balls on their behalf with the dates of their Captaincy engraved thereon'. Meanwhile, in October 1879, the Captain announced that a petition to the Town Council asking for 'the presentation of a new Silver Club similar to those given in 1744 and 1811' had been successful. On 26th February, 1880, a Club Dinner was held in the Windsor Hotel, Edinburgh, at which the Lord Provost, Mr. Thomas J. Boyd, and other members of the Town Council were guests, and the third Silver Club was presented to the Captain, Mr. W. J. Mure. The gift of the third Club marked a special act of generosity on the part of the Town Council since the Company were no longer their tenants at Leith. Throughout its history, however, the Honourable Company has continued to enjoy the goodwill of the City. The third Club is all but complete and the continued favour of the Town Council is awaited with a mixture of confidence and anxiety.

There was also a close and continuing association between the Honourable Company and the North Berwick Golf Club which came to notice last century. The North Berwick Club had started in 1832 and a number

of other Edinburgh Clubs, including the Honourable Company (possibly
with the summer holidays in mind), paid an annual subscription towards
its upkeep. At a General Meeting of the Honourable Company held in
April 1882, approval was given to a request from Mr. P. Brodie, North
Berwick, that the Honourable Company should increase its contribution
from ten to fifteen guineas per annum. A request for a further increase
from fifteen guineas to £25 in April 1885 was received less favourably.
The Honourable Company then suggested that a new Green Committee
should be formed at North Berwick to take charge of the Golfing Green,
consisting of members of the present Committee and a representative
from each other Club subscribing to the North Berwick Club. This
proposal does not seem to have gone with much of a swing: no acknow-
ledgement was received from North Berwick, and the subscription was
cancelled.

Growing congestion at Musselburgh, with four Clubs playing almost
concurrently, made a move to a more spacious location increasingly
likely, but for long there was no agreement that any disturbance was
necessary. The Links were perhaps not on the most attractive part of
the coastline and lacked any particular features which might command
affection. But they were hallowed with the memory of mighty matches
in the days of Lord President Inglis, Lord Rutherfurd Clark and other
members of the Bench and Bar who, then as now, did not find that their
judicial duties at Parliament House occupied all their physical and mental
energy. The Clubhouse had been built by the Honourable Company,
appreciable sums had been spent on keeping it in repair, and there were
those who thought that the companionship of the Links, crowded as they
were, the Clubhouse, and an occasional sharpener in the Musselburgh
taverns, adequate for their needs.

A recurring feature of the Honourable Company's history becomes
apparent at Musselburgh. The matches which the members recalled most
vividly were played against each other: not against other Clubs: and not
by means of stroke play for prizes. In the Rev. John Kerr's succinct
words – 'The Honourable Company, it may here be stated, is almost, it
not absolutely, the only club which never plays for pots and pans.'
There are two meetings in the year, in the spring and autumn, at which
the only prizes are the scratch medals. For the rest of the year, match
play is the thing and, however parochial or insular they may seem to the
outside world, the members are content with the rewards to be derived

JOHN TAYLOR
Captain 1807 and 1808, 1814 and 1815, 1823-25, and 1828

from the rigours of the game and from overcoming the adversary. This attitude is reflected in the importance attached to the Bett Book which, however, requires elaboration later.

Meanwhile, as late as 1890, a complete removal from Musselburgh was not being contemplated, although it was decided that expenditure on the Clubhouse and Links should be 'reduced to the minimum'. The next year the Clubhouse was still reported to be in good condition and it was not until the Winter Business Meeting held in Dowell's Rooms, Edinburgh, on 4th November, 1891, that a motion by Mr. Robert Clark, to dispose of the Clubhouse in favour of smaller accommodation, started the train of events that led to the departure for Muirfield. Two days later, the last Honourable Company medal at Musselburgh was won by Mr. A. Stuart with 80; Mr. J. E. Laidlay being runner-up four strokes behind.

Those who wanted to stay behind did not lack spirit or an ability to invoke the rules and see that the proposals which they did not like were properly obstructed on the merits. At various meetings held during the following year, a lively rearguard action was fought against selling the Clubhouse. Eventually the Committee were instructed 'before closing the Club House at Musselburgh to provide accommodation at Musselburgh for such members of the Club as wish to play there at a cost not exceeding £150 per annum'. The Clubhouse was disposed of in March 1893 for £800 and an annual subsidy of £150 was to be provided for members of the Honourable Company to enable them to use 100 club boxes and have all the privileges of a Club called 'The New Club, Musselburgh', except participation in competitions and any share in management. The exact terms of the agreement are set out in the Minutes of a Committee Meeting held on 4th March, 1893. Thereafter the talk was all of Muirfield.

Shortly before the move from Musselburgh, Sir Walter Simpson had published *The Art of Golf*. This remarkable sportsman, who on his own admission was a poor cricketer, a hopeless billiard player and an execrable shot and who had taken up golf on doctor's orders when over sixty years of age, was a man whose wit and sensibility were soon recognised by the Honourable Company. To them he dedicated his classic manual 'humbly as a golfer, proudly as their Captain, gratefully for merry meetings and cordially without permission'.

In this slightly ironic, but sometimes remarkably scientific, handbook of instruction, Simpson has some penetrating remarks on the art of

D

foursomes which, throughout its history, has always been the Honourable
Company's favourite form of the game:

> Some particularly tender-hearted golfers play better in foursomes than
> in singles, because in the latter they are apt to have their bowels of
> compassion moved and their game made loose by the grumblings and
> lamentation of the adversary whom they have got well in hand.
> Playing a foursome will not lessen his dread of the other side when
> down, but it will prevent the merciful man from being moved by pity.
> The wailing, the discontent about the odds, the depreciation of stymes,
> the harping on the flukiness of long putts holed, his good luck, their bad
> luck, will not melt his heart and soften his muscle. Between him and
> them is one nearer and dearer – his partner. It is not selfish to crush the
> enemy; it is duty – duty to the partner. What are the tears of two
> enemies to the joy of one friend?

He is also pretty profound on putting:

> When a putter is waiting his turn to hole-out a putt of one or two feet
> in length, on which the match hangs at the last hole, it is of vital
> importance that he think of nothing. At this supreme moment he ought
> studiously to fill his mind with vacancy. He must not even allow himself
> the consolation of religion. He must not prepare himself to accept the
> gloomy face of his partner and the derisive delight of his adversaries
> with Christian resignation should he miss.

Should he sink his putt 'It is not well to say, "I couldn't have missed it".
Silence is best. The pallid cheek and trembling lip belie such braggadocio.'
The last Winter Medal at Musselburgh was one of the few outright wins
recorded by Alexander Stuart, Advocate. For long he was the supreme
golfer to emerge from the Bench and Bar at Parliament House, and the
esteem in which he was held by his fellow members was marked by his
election to the Captaincy in the crucial year, 1892, to superintend the
Club's reconstruction at Muirfield. He cannot have been much over
thirty when he was elected Captain. He remained a member for seventy-
two years and during all that time there was no more popular or engaging
figure at Musselburgh and at Muirfield. The portrait, showing him in the
Captain's evening-dress, which hangs in the Smoking Room, is convinc-
ing evidence of the genial, quizzical sense of humour recorded in contemporary reports. As a competitor it was perhaps his misfortune to
coincide with two other great members of the Honourable Company:
Leslie Balfour-Melville and J. E. Laidlay: and his main achievement was,
perhaps, to win the first Irish Open championship in 1892.   The Rev.

John Kerr judged Stuart to have a very finished and beautiful style of play and, on occasion, 'his "swipes" and his "approach shots" were unblemished', but, possibly because of other preoccupations as a politician and a Highland sportsman, he did not quite attain the same monotonous success as his two distinguished contemporaries.

From 1882 the name of Leslie Balfour-Melville (originally Balfour) appears with great regularity in the medal winners' lists. He won six gold, and three silver, medals of the Honourable Company and was to become Amateur Champion in 1895. It is open to dispute – a dispute never to be settled – whether he was a better golfer than Laidlay, but he was certainly more versatile. Captain of the Honourable Company in 1902-3, he was also Captain of the Royal and Ancient in 1906, and represented Scotland at golf, rugby and cricket as well as being Scottish Lawn Tennis Champion: a record which is never likely to be equalled. Those who saw him play said that he seemed 'all muscle'. Photographs show an unusually determined face with a strong jaw: he was quite imperturbable with an unfailing nerve for the big occasion. Not for him a new-fangled iron putter. It was reported that his heavily weighted wooden implement seemed to be soled with brass. Lesser athletes can only look on his works and seek to emulate them.

But the dominating figure of the last decade in the nineteenth century was undoubtedly John Ernest Laidlay (1860-1919). Born at Seacliffe, he went to school at Loretto and so was early to be found on the adjacent Links at Musselburgh. He generously acknowledged that one of the Musselburgh professionals, Bob Ferguson, taught him the rudiments which he thereafter applied with conspicuous success. Jack White, who caddied for him before they played together in the 1895 Open, was another friend. Laidlay won the Amateur Championship twice in 1889 and 1891, beating Leslie Balfour-Melville in the first final and H. H. Hilton in the second. He was runner-up to Willie Auchterlonie in the 1893 Open Championship, two strokes behind the winner. In a long golfing career, when he sometimes seemed incapable of losing, he played for Scotland against England in ten successive years and won ten gold medals at Musselburgh – a number which he later equalled at Muirfield. His scoring feats are difficult to evaluate nowadays when courses have changed, although all his contemporaries were impressed by the staccato way in which he would fire off a series of threes and twos. He was the first golfer of eminence to use the overlapping grip, now called after

Vardon, but his style was not held up for imitation, and he played every shot, including his putts, off the left foot in a highly individual way. He used a light cleek on the green and his putting style resembled a batsman playing forward to a well-pitched ball. Like Balfour-Melville, he was also a good cricketer and played for Scotland against Yorkshire. But, as a golfer, he was a giant.

The Links at Musselburgh, where golf is still played, are worth more than a cursory glance. The general ambiance of the links is consistent with the historical and descriptive account of the conception of a course published by the Royal and Ancient Club in 1857:

> The Golfing Course is arbitrary in form; sometimes circular, sometimes oblong but generally stretching irregularly in a winding direction. The best site for a golfing ground is by the sea shore and we find nearly all of the Scottish Links so situated. A sandy soil does not encourage the thick and luxuriant growth of grass which an earthy soil does, thus the turf is easily trodden down to velvety smoothness merely by the pressure of the players' feet. At intervals of time nomadic flocks of sheep aid in keeping the herbage down so that the course is always fit for the niceties of the game without any special attention. Still the theatre of our scientific passtime is by no means a Bowling Green; the course proper alone has this trim appearance. On each side bristle all kinds of furzy horrors – whins, thick tufted heath and many other situation of distress for a wandering ball. The course [presumably the fairway] on a good Links is not wider, on an average, than 30 to 60 yards, nor is golfing, even on this cleared space, altogether plain sailing. The surface is dotted over at frequent intervals with sandy holes, technically called bunkers, from two to six feet deep, of irregular forms and sizes, whilst here and there a whin is left in a likely place to intercept the unwary stroke. Then there is the inequalities of the ground – a hillock here, an abrupt rift there – to vary the play.

> Some Links again have more the appearance of parks, the whins (tough old bushes too) have ceased to mark with their yellow bloom the heathery margin of the course; the bunkers have degenerated from stiff golfing hazards into a resort for children with wheelbarrows, spades and agricultural propensities. To complete the taming of such a links the reader has only to picture to himself the daily inroads of the kine appertaining unto some economic milkman – a score or two of nursery-maids – a few rinks of quoits – and, sprinkling the scene with washer-women, he will easily see that in such a region the royal and ancient game of Golf is in imminent danger of dying a natural death, or at all events, of being deprived of its most delightful perils.

Over the course, at distances from each other from 80 to 400 yards are bored small circular holes about four inches in diameter. These holes are placed on specially smooth tables of turf called putting greens, for there the nicer strokes of the game are played. When they have been played to for some little time these holes are shifted a few yards, as well to preserve the green from too much rubbing as to vary the play by changing the lie of the ground in the short game.

Originally the Musselburgh course had seven holes; another was added in 1838; and the full complement of nine was opened for play in 1870 when the total length was about 2,800 yards. The first three holes went from the Racecourse Grandstand to Formans Inn at the eastern end of the Links. These holes measured 350, 430 and 450 yards and were named 'The Graves', 'Linkfield' and 'Formans' respectively and were bogey fives. All three holes called for long straight driving between the road on the right, and, on the left, bunkers and gorse. On reaching Formans, which still flourishes, the next hole went north towards the sea (The Sea Hole) and was 180 yards in length. It was at this stage that the turf, which had been rather clay-like, changed to true seaside texture. The fifth and sixth holes went westward adjacent to the sea – occasionally too close for comfort. The feature of the fifth (400 yards) was a cross bunker aptly named 'Pandemonium', or 'Pandy' for short, which was faced with wooden sleepers that lasted until the late 1920s. The hole was called 'The Table' after its plateau green. The sixth, of 346 yards, was called 'The Bathing Coach' after the old coach, or shelter, which was provided for bathers to change in. A splendid Victorian daguerreotype of bewhiskered bathers is evoked by the name of this hole. 'The High Hole', of 220 yards, looked innocent enough but it was difficult to get the ball to run true to the green. The eighth, the odoriferous 'Gas Hole' (270 yards), in the north-west corner of the course, was a bogey four, as were the sixth and seventh. The 'Home Hole' (ninth), which was a bogey three of some 150 yards, still exists as the first hole on the Links today, and Loretto boys who still play there can testify that, even with all modern accessories and a reasonable putting surface, it is not an easy three.

The last three holes on the Old Links were the scene of one of the most stirring finishes in the history of the Open Championship when, in 1883, Bob Ferguson, a local professional, had to do each of these holes in three to tie for the Title; and did it, watched by a large, mixed audience:

It was growing quite dusk and from one side to the other the course was lined with a dense mass of spectators, gentlemen of learning and top hatted from Edinburgh, the modern Athens, shoulder to shoulder with grimy miners who had climed from the bowels of the earth to see the play.

Bob Ferguson lost the play-off to W. Fernie of Dumfries, but he had won on each of the three previous years.

During their stay at Musselburgh, the Honourable Company sponsored and ran six Open Championships. Apart from Ferguson and Fernie, the winners were Mungo Park, from the famous golfing family of that name; Jamie Anderson of St. Andrews; D. Brown of Musselburgh; and W. Park, Junior; the last named having the best aggregate with 155 for 36 holes. Willie Park also held the record for the course of 32. As far as the Honourable Company was concerned, Mr. J. E. Laidlay's score of 79 and 80 for two rounds to win the Gold Medal in 1887 was the best recorded by a member and was well up to Open championship standard.

CHAPTER IV

THE BOX-FRAMED SALON

The Rev. John Kerr, writing from Dirleton in 1896, argued that the Honourable Company's decision to move to Muirfield 'should not be considered as an accidental circumstance, but as a natural stage in the evolution of golf in this part of Scotland'. He went on to recall that the Lords of Session 'played where they worked, or close by, with their brother lawyers on Leith Links. During the winter season many of our country noblemen resided in the metropolis and with the Lords of Session disported themselves over the same course. At that time our golfers left East Lothian and golfed with their Edinburgh friends at Leith. At the present time Edinburgh seeks her golf, especially in the summer season, in East Lothian, thus reversing the position.' This is a more specious claim than most of the reverend sportsman's propositions, and it conveniently omits any reference to the Honourable Company's staging at Musselburgh or to the spread of the game to those of slightly humbler origin. Nor was the decision to move to East Lothian by any means unanimous. The first discussions with the Edinburgh Town Council had been directed towards the Honourable Company investing the Braid Hills, but, for reasons perhaps more obvious now than they were then, the scheme was soon dropped.

The first site to be seriously considered was a stretch of ground at Hedderwick, on the Tyne estuary opposite the Earl of Haddington's residence at Tyninghame House. Looked at today, the ground seems fairly flat and featureless and there need be no regret that this proposal was not adopted. But it nearly was, although it was clear from an early stage that the North British Railway Company would be characteristically difficult about improving the Belton Ford siding on the main line. The Captain (Colonel J. W. Anderson of Bourhouse) proposed the acquisition at a meeting on 9th June, 1890, in the Windsor Hotel, Edinburgh, but there were doubts about the distance from the Capital. Craigielaw, to the west of Aberlady, near the present Kilspindie course, was also considered, but the proprietor, the Earl of Wemyss and March, was not in favour. Hedderwick remained the most likely solution until two new proposals, each with very active sponsors, emerged.

A month after the Windsor Hotel meeting, Mr. Henry W. Hope of Luffness offered land at Saltcoats, roughly the area now occupied by the Luffness New Golf Club. On the same day, Mr. B. Hall Blyth, an ex-Captain, reported favourably on a possible site at Muirfield. The Minutes, objective as they are, do not entirely conceal the sharp clash of personalities or the controversy which ensued. Mr. Hope argued, with some reason, that professional advice should be sought before any irrevocable decision was taken. Mr. Hope had been a member since 1868, and Mr. Stair Gillon shrewdly observed that 'his fellow members may have been apprehensive of his benevolent despotism'. The members were also diffident about opposing any of Mr. Hall Blyth's proposals for long, and it seems very likely that his potent presentation was a decisive factor.

Hall Blyth (Captain, 1880–81; Recorder, 1888–96; and a Trustee from 1894 onwards) was a civil engineer by profession and, though keen, was never a scratch player. He triumphed in the famous cross-country match in 1880, against Willie Campbell, which was played from Point Garry, North Berwick, to the High Hole at Gullane. Campbell opted for the shore line and played over North Berwick, Archerfield and the ground that eventually became Muirfield, before reaching Gullane. Hall Blyth elected to play on an inland route through Dirleton and, although longer, this was much the simpler course. Hall Blyth won easily over the six mile distance and his opponent came early to grief on the rocks.

Hall Blyth served continuously on numerous committees concerned with Golf Clubs throughout East Lothian and he usually got his way. A tall, powerfully built man, he had a loud voice in which he boomed confident opinions and defied challenge. He wore a Dragoon's moustache and affected something of the air of a martinet. To see him, attired in checks almost as loud as his voice, referee a championship match and hear his resonant rulings was said to be unforgettable. His appetite was famous. He used to apply the gouge to the Stilton cheese with the same vigour that he brandished his niblick in a bunker – leaving a similar cavity. But he also seems to have inspired some admiration – and perhaps some reluctant affection. His services in acquiring and preparing the course at Muirfield were suitably recorded in a special Minute of 4th April, 1894, and he, more than anyone else, is responsible for the present clubhouse and the Muirfield Green.

The Honourable Company were about to move from one racecourse to another. The 'Hundred Acre Field' also called the 'Howes' on the Archerfield estate, which was to become tthe new golf course, was the site of the annual East Lothian races, and a number of famous horses, including Lanercost who won the first Cambridgeshire, were trained there. In 1832 an outbreak of cholera in the city lead to the Edinburgh Race Meeting being transferred to the 'Howes' – Ballochmyle winning one of the races only to drop dead at the post, not far from the present last hole.

The lease negotiated with the laird, Mr. Hamilton Ogilvy, gave the Club a twenty-one year lease at £120 a year. For the first time the Honourable Company had undisputed control over their links. They also had good access from Edinburgh by way of Drem railway station or, before long, by the new Longniddry–Gullane branch line. Stair Gillon was in near-libellous form in describing the pleasures of a journey by the new route:

> How delightful it was to feel the jolt as the London line was left and the little train floated at the back of the Gosford policies through fields fat with corn and pheasants, to find a station in a field styled 'Aberlady' and then resume by the back of the Luffness policies to the region few of us knew as Saltcoats where there might be a stop at some planks for New Luffness members, then puffing on to the station beneath the shadow of the amazing pagoda which did and possibly does duty for a hotel and is a tribute to the taste of the Dirleton baroness and her advisers, worthy of that culminating cube of vulgarity on the very top of Gullane Hill. It was a walk of three-quarters of a mile from the platform to the front door of Muirfield. The immediate result of the opening was that Gullane Station was besieged with boys, to whose solicitations it was proper to turn a deaf ear (bags were not so heavy then and some of us kept our clubs at the Club House), although this was by no means what happened always.

The smooth way in which the acquisition arrangements were completed owed much to the Honorary Secretaries, Mr. John Bruce, a rather shadowy figure, and Mr. D. R. Kemp. It seems clear that Mr. Kemp, Secretary to the Union Bank in Edinburgh, kept a vigilant eye on all the financial arrangements and he received a silver salver and Honorary Life Membership when he moved South on preferment to a superior post in London. He was succeeded in 1894 by Mr. A. G. G. Asher, W.S., a distinguished athlete, triple 'blue' and a keen golfer very much in the Muirfield tradition.

But we must not overlook the rites that marked the transfer of the Lares et Penates when the Muirfield Green (still only 16 holes) was opened for play on 3rd May, 1891. It rained intermittently throughout the day, heavy showers stopping only long enough to lure the unwary out for a second drenching. Colonel Anderson, the Captain, for some inexplicable reason, was not present at the opening, and the votive fillet was assumed for the occasion by a veteran ex-Captain, Sir Alexander Kinloch (1867), who drove the first ball with suitable solemnity and enough skill to avoid derision. The spectators then watched Mr. A. Stuart play his own ball against the better ball of Mr. Hall Blyth and Mr. F. V. Hagart. Mr. Stuart was normally much the best of the three, but on this occasion he found, as others have done since, that playing the best ball of two opponents is mathematically more difficult than appears, and he was defeated.

Since the new Clubhouse could scarcely be ready in time, the company, about 130 strong, who had assembled for the ceremonies, were entertained to luncheon in a large marquee which had been erected on the edge of Muirfield Green. Mr. Marshall, the leading caterer of the time, provided victuals at 5s. a head, the balance being found by the Honourable Company. After luncheon, Sir Alexander Kinloch, in proposing the health of the proprietors, said that at Muirfield they should 'escape from the gamin with the cleek, from the nursemaid with the perambulator, and from the bailie who would shut up and open roads without regard to the enjoyment of the game'. After a suitably fulsome reply by Mr. Hamilton Ogilvy, who proposed 'The Honourable Company of Edinburgh Golfers and success to Muirfield Green', the sun appeared unexpectedly and play was resumed: but not for long. Heavy rain returned and the company of pilgrims, now slightly steaming, returned to Edinburgh by special train from Drem, leaving at half-past five.

The Minutes of the period are strangely silent about the arrangements for laying out the new Elysium. It was as though the Olympian members of the Honourable Company were justified in expecting Jupiter himself to provide a new course as soon as they were ready to move from Mussel-burgh. In more mundane terms, it is recorded elsewhere in this book that the work was carried out by David Plenderleith, working to Tom Morris's plan. Meanwhile, the Honourable Company proceeded with complete unconcern – and, to our eyes, very incautiously – without taking the trouble to appoint a Greenkeeper. But, on 13th July, 1891, those dedicated members, Mr. Hall Blyth and Mr. Andrew Stuart (Captain for the next two years), were appointed to form a Green Committee. They received no further instructions and it was apparently left to them both to supervise the preparation of the Muirfield Green and to devise all the arrangements for housing the Open Championship in the following year.

Even allowing for the rudimentary nature, by modern standards, of the preparations required, it was a notable achievement, to get the course in order for a major championship in the compass of a single year – especially bearing in mind the slightly dilettante way in which the Honourable Company set about it. From contemporary records, there is no doubt that, apart from Andrew Kirkaldy's caustic comment that Muirfield was 'just an auld watter meedie', there were few, if any, complaints about the face which the Honourable Company presented to the outside world when it first declared itself open for championship visitors in 1892. The Muirfield championships as a whole are described in separate chapters, but a mention of the competitors in the 1892 event sets the Muirfield activities in the general perspective of the golfing scene. The importance ascribed to the event, in East Lothian at least, is shown by an entry in the log-book kept by the Headmaster of Dirleton School:

> Intended that those who had passed the Fifth standard or reached their 14th birthday might absent themselves for that day. About a dozen of those who had neither were also absent. Made them do all they had missed the following day.

This was the first occasion when the championship consisted of four rounds – thirty-six holes on each day. Mr. Horace G. Hutchison would have won under the old conditions: with rounds of 74 and 78 he led by three strokes at the end of the first day. His third round, however, was a disastrous one of 86 – 14 more than the new record for the course of 72 set by Mr. H. H. Hilton from Hoylake. Hilton finished in 74 for a grand total of 305, three strokes ahead of another famous amateur, Mr. John Ball, Jun., who shared second place with the professionals Hugh Kirkaldy and A. Herd. Since then Muirfield has remained on the championship rota.

The Honourable Company were scarcely so successful with their Clubhouse. It was evident from the start that it lacked any architectural distinction and, despite repeated additions, it was nearly always too small. It was the custom to cast some obloquy on Hall Blyth who was responsible for the plans and to recall, as though an afterthought, that he was an engineer, not an architect. Certainly, Hall Blyth prepared the plans and persuaded the Committee to accept the lowest tender, from an Edinburgh builder, for £1,574: this proved to be a bad bargain as, three years later, the dining-hall was discovered to be infected with dry rot. But it is perhaps scarcely fair to stigmatise Hall Blyth too much for his 'box-framed salon'. His taste was simply that of a man of his time, and few of the clubhouses built in the late Victorian era were much more than licensed changing shacks. Golfers everywhere seemed determined to perpetuate the tavernous origins of their club premises.

It would accordingly have been astonishing if Hall Blyth had devised, or commissioned, anything to rival the elegant austerity which distinguishes the outlines of High Walls (now called Greywalls) nearby. High Walls, which was soon to be built a short distance to the east of the clubhouse, is one of Sir Edwin Lutyens's most successful country house designs. It adds lustre to the Muirfield scene.

But, almost by accident, the Clubhouse displayed some merit of its own. The Rev. John Kerr enthused over it as 'the most handsome and commodious in the country' with a central hall 'in which the portraits of club heroes are displayed'. Stair Gillon, too, reflecting on mortality as he gazed round the brass plates on the individual boxes round the hall, was moved, for all his usual asperity, to ask, 'What greater ambition can a man have in life than some day to join the Honourable Company?' Perhaps he realised that it is the view from within, rather than the outside appearance of, the Clubhouse that matters.

Hall Blyth deployed what he was pleased to call an Elizabethan design with a half-timbered main gable. It would be interesting to know exactly what he thought he was doing when he introduced this exotic pattern to the Hundred Acre field. With the passage of time, and modified by subsequent extensions, the clubhouse now harmonises well with the landscape and the growing number of buildings on either side; but the original effect must have been startling. Much use was made of local materials and the stone was mostly obtained from the Rattlebags Quarry at East Fenton. With some extravagance, the corners and facings of the windows were made of red freestone, specially brought from Nevat Quarry, Cumberland. Originally the building consisted of seven bedrooms for members, the usual kitchen and office premises, a small committee/ dining-room for those staying in the clubhouse and, as the only really striking feature, the Great Hall used as a dining-room at weekends and on other populous occasions. Here Hall Blyth's engineer's eye helped him. He built a long, narrow room (44′ x 25′) with a ceiling of quite exceptional height. Large windows at both the north and south ends ensure an uninterrupted view of the course and welcome the sunlight. This part of his plan, at least, satisfied the aspirations of the Honourable Company. The lighting has always been particularly successful, and the rays of the sun produce a spectacular effect when seen through the glass barrel, at the south end of the room, which is full (at the beginning of the day) of whisky. In more recent times, the amber-coloured barrel has had, along-side it, another one containing the more pellucid liquid distilled from the juice of the juniper. Two glass barrels, full of excisable liquor, are still preserved in the dining-room and their appearance, as well as their content, make anyone's first visit memorable.

Within four years of the opening of the Clubhouse, in April 1895, Mr. George Dalziel, W.S., a leading member of the time, persuaded the Honourable Company that more dressing accommodation was needed, and this turned out to cost as much as the original clubhouse. Hall Blyth again provided the plans, with little more distinction than his earlier ones. By now, however, as the members sat round the fire in the dining-room – on the club fender brought from the Carlton Club in London – they began to reflect that their finances were not in a very healthy state. The Committee felt unable to entertain an offer by the National Telephone Company to provide a telephone for the Club at a fee of £10 per annum, but it was not long before the members found it necessary to accept this proposition. By 1898 the Club debt was £7,500, and the following year it was decided to impose a levy of £5 on each member. At the same time, green fees for visitors, at the modest rate of 1s. per day, were introduced. The levy raised £2,000, and the Club's indebtedness to the bank was reduced by £1,800. For some time to come the Honourable Company thought that they were tolerably solvent, and overdue repairs were put in hand.

In addition to those already mentioned, the great Muirfield names of this period included Sir Henry Cook, Messrs. Andrew Graham Murray (later Viscount Dunedin), A. R. Paterson, J. W. Brodie, C. J. G. Paterson, David Lyall, Pat Murray, W. J. Mure and Hugh Patten, who took over the duties of Honorary Secretary from A. G. G. Asher in 1899. Patten was the gentlest but most efficient of secretaries and excited a great deal of admiration and goodwill among the Honourable Company.

The great golfing figure at the beginning of the century was, beyond argument, Robert Maxwell who was gradually taking over from his heroic predecessors, Laidlay and Balfour-Melville. His record was formidable. Amateur Champion in 1903 and 1909, he was leading amateur in the Open Championship in 1902 and 1903 : and he played for Scotland against England for eight years running. In his time he won eighty-four medals, including twenty from the Honourable Company and nine from the Royal and Ancient. He also won the St. George's Challenge Cup at Sandwich. Despite this impressive public record, he was by instinct a private, rather than a public, golfer and, although the Scottish public recognised him to be the successor to Freddie Tait as the leading golfer in the country, it is doubtful if their hearts warmed to him as much as to his predecessor. He won both his Amateur Championships at Muirfield where he was, as near as might be, invincible. He might well have won elsewhere, for at his prime he was a really tremendous player, but he was happiest playing in East Lothian. After the war, when he won the Military Cross serving with the Royal Scots, he played golf only with his friends, some of whom can still recall how impressed they were to see him playing a cleek shot boring into the wind, straight on the flag.

As an administrator he was equally famous at Muirfield. From 1906 onwards, he was seldom off the Committee and, as Captain in 1912 and 1913, he encouraged the Club to 'consider acquiring more land to the north and building a course more worthy of its prestige'. When the ground became available after the war, it was he who advised the golf architects – Mr. Colt and Mr. Simpson – on the lay-out and alterations. There was not a championship at Muirfield from 1906 until 1948 when his advice was not sought. He was one of the chief movers in suggesting that the Royal and Ancient should take over the management of the Amateur and Open Championships, and he was a member of the first Royal and Ancient Championship Committee. Robert Maxwell died in 1950 at the age of 74. In the Smoking Room at Muirfield hangs a portrait of him by Stanley Cursiter, The Queen's painter and limner in Scotland. It shows a pleasant contemplative figure, and is rightly entitled 'Portrait of a Golfer'.

The Minutes from the turn of the century to the outbreak of the First World War (kept by Mr. Hugh Patten and then by Mr. J. C. Couper) are largely concerned with day-to-day trivia, with routine questions about building and furnishing, and with piecemeal alterations to the course. During all the time spent at Muirfield, the Club had been admirably served by three stewards and their families: Mr. George Fitzjohn, a dignified Victorian figure who had accompanied the Club in their move from Musselburgh; Mr. Pinner (1897–1902), who contrived an eminently satisfactory cuisine; and Mr. Henry Burroughs, who affected a slight hauteur in his dealing with the members. They are all remembered for their discreet, unfailing and wholly effective contribution to the welfare and enjoyment of the Honourable Company.

During the first decade of the twentieth century, the members took a growing delight in their new course. But the arrival of the Haskell ball soon disturbed any complacency that the new links would do for all time. Even average golfers, rejoicing in the greater length which was possible with the Haskell, were beginning to demand longer courses. Length was becoming a matter of prestige. The reaction of the public to the three Open and two Amateur Championships at Muirfield (in 1901, 1906 and 1912, and in 1903 and 1909 respectively) emphasised beyond the possibility of argument that, if the Club was to maintain the reputation of the Muirfield Green, some of the structural shortcomings would have to be remedied. While a more capacious clubhouse was needed, it was also recognised that a more ambitious and testing lay-out of the course was an absolute necessity; otherwise the reclame that had survived since the days of John Rattray would be subject to some painful erosion. In the event, substantial and beneficial improvements were made to the clubhouse, but a recasting of the links, though the subject of much discussion – particularly about the offending Northern wall – had to wait till after the First World War.

Security of tenure had been a matter of growing concern since the lease of the links and clubhouse land was due to expire in 1912. The Committee, however, with uncharacteristic prescience, negotiated a new lease well in advance; in 1905 the original one was cancelled and a new one at a rent of £300 a year, to take effect for twenty-one years, was negotiated. The Honourable Company were thus safe until at least 1926. Alterations to the clubhouse were becoming imperative, and Mr. J. M. Dick Peddie, an architect and member of the Club, was made responsible for detailed plans. The first plan provided for some modest additions to the changing rooms at a cost of £1,700, but no provision was made for a Smoking Room. Fortunately, better counsel prevailed and an additional

£1,000 was authorised for a Smoking Room to be ready for occupation
by December 1906. A further sum was subsequently allocated for
panelling the Smoking Room in yellow pine up to a height of 4′ 6″.
Double rows of boxes, brass labelled and still funereal in appearance,
were to be erected in the new dressing-room and on each side of the
corridor. But, happily, Mr. Patrick Murray (Captain 1908–9) took exception to the inclusion of boxes in the new Smoking Room – for which
subsequent members of the Honourable Company must tip their caps in
grateful obeisance.

The new Smoking Room, perhaps from its cube-like shape, proved
from the start to be warm and welcoming. So far as any room which is
furnished with club leather chairs and small round tables can offer an
elegant appearance, elegance it has. The walls are in good proportion to
accommodate the Honourable Company's Raeburns and other massive
portraits, reproduced in our illustrations, together with replicas of the
original Rules. The space inside the large window provides a stamping
ground from which the members, particularly at weekends, can watch
their colleagues toiling thirstily up the last fairway: scabrous comments
abound and wagers are made on the remote possibility of the last few
shots being properly executed – wagers whose existence is surmised by the
players as they address the ball for their last pitch. It is in the Smoking
Room that the afternoon's matches are arranged and, with the lightest of
reins, the Captain will ensure that everyone who wants a game has one
arranged.

During this time there was also a growing volume of correspondence
on the Club's relations with the Championship Committees; with neigh-
bours, like the tenant of High Walls; and with neighbouring clubs about
caddies, wages and permits to play. Permits authorising visiting clubs to
have the privilege of playing on the links had originally been granted as a
matter of courtesy and deriving from some old association. But, as more
golfing societies were formed, this came to be regarded as a profitable
source of revenue. Among those who have been allowed to muster their
own competitions at Muirfield have been the Bench and Bar Golfing
Society, Edinburgh Corporation, Edinburgh High Constables and the
golfing societies from the Scottish Public Schools – whose brave appearance latterly in the annual blood-letting for the Halford-Hewitt Cup at
Deal may owe something to practising the necessary commital attitudes at
Muirfield.

ALEXANDER STUART
Captain 1892 and 1893

In the last few Edwardian years before the howitzers started firing, golf was still a developing game. The different trajectory which was possible with the Haskell ball had given a new impetus. Perhaps because the game was no longer associated with any particular stratum of society, there is not the impression that the pre-1914 era marked any kind of Indian summer for golfers, as has sometimes been remarked about other games. Two contemporary developments can, however, be noted – Sunday play, and the admission of ladies.

When it is recalled that the proposal to allow Sunday play on the Old Course at St. Andrews aroused the strongest passions after the Second World War, it is all the more surprising that Sunday play was allowed at Muirfield from 1903 onwards. Admittedly, the conditions were different. The possibility of encroachment by the public at St. Andrews – or, for that matter, at Musselburgh or North Berwick – meant that the spectacle of golfers exercising themselves on the Sabbath would have aroused strong complaints, not confined to Sabbatarians. At Muirfield, however, there was sufficient privacy to allow Sunday play almost without discussion. The legislative solution was exemplary. In 1903 members were simply asked not to introduce visitors on Sundays; the access gate was kept locked; and play proceeded peacefully from then on. Sunday play was a light-hearted affair and there were no caddies. 'No waiting; no onlookers; just peewits and the ripple of the "rough" in the wind or the boom of a steamer's siren in a fog. What did it matter if the rabbits had visited the shaggy putting greens and left tangible proof of their trespass?' But the Honourable Company, perhaps realising their good fortune, adhered to the 'no visitor' rule on Sundays and, as late as 1909, the now venerable Mr. Hall Blyth was prevented from entertaining a party of guests.

The Honourable Company have, on occasion, been represented as a misogynous society, though with little reason, as is apparent from the complete lack of prohibition on ladies playing on the links, except on Medal days. It is true that there is no ladies' section, nor Ladies Golf Union tees, but the records show that the names of lady visitors have been entered in a special book kept in the Committee Room since February 1904 and – somewhat unusually – there are no particular days in the week when ladies' play is forbidden. As early as 1914, the Scottish Ladies Golfing Association held their championship meeting at Muirfield and were also granted the use of the clubhouse; all this long before

E

post-war emancipation. Since then there have been occasional, though admittedly infrequent, national competitions, including that for the Curtis Cup (British Isles *v.* USA) in 1952, and the Vagliano Cup (British Isles and the Rest of Europe) in 1963.

During the First World War Muirfield, like all other courses, was really on a care and maintenance basis. Mr. C. J. G. Paterson of Castle Huntly, in the Carse of Gowrie, became Captain in 1914 and held office throughout the war until he handed over to Mr. A. G. G. Asher in 1919. His tenure of office was a joyless one, and the Honourable Company owe much to him and the Honorary Secretary, Mr. John (later Sir John) C. Couper, and the Committee members who helped to keep the Club together. Mr. Paterson was also known as a keen Lorettonian, and the connection between the school and the Honourable Company has always been close. The Musselburgh Medal, played for by the Honourable Company, as its second medal at the Autumn Meeting, was presented to the Club by Lorettonian members in 1908. During the war, Medal and Club Dinners were abandoned; the Clubhouse and contents were insured against aircraft risks; and, in 1915, the Committee 'considered it advisable also to insure against bombardment' – which, even then, must have been a fairly remote contingency. The Amateur Championship, due to take place at Muirfield in 1915, was cancelled, and the Royal and Ancient intimated that it would still take place at Muirfield when play was resumed. On an optimistic note, prudent management kept the Club's finances in a healthy condition, and during the war years the Club debt was reduced by nearly one-third.

CHAPTER V

THE MUIRFIELD GREEN

In the early years of their existence, it is the activities of the Gentlemen Golfers and their attitudes, imperious, generous, vexatious or hospitable, to one another that are sometimes of most interest. But they did play golf. They have always been obsessed with the delights of internecine combat with one another, while trophies (apart from the Spring and Autumn Medals), handicaps and stroke play have little part in their existence. It has been alleged that, in the unlikely event of a member entering the Smoking Room before lunch on a Sunday to announce modestly that he had gone round in under par, he would provoke only the frosty riposte – 'Why?' Companionable contest is the objective, and to this end the Honourable Company have always been proud of their links for their own use, for that of visiting societies, and for the periodic national championships that take place there. The earlier courses at Leith and Musselburgh are of historic, but now mainly of transient, interest. With the arrival at the hundred acre field at Muirfield, however, it is a different story.

The setting is one to please the aesthete equally with the athlete. The eye goes first eastwards to the volcanic mound of North Berwick Law and the gnarled wood of Archerfield which landscapes the view towards the sand-dunes in the north. Archerfield was the setting of Robert Louis Stevenson's melodramatic novella *The Pavilion on the Links* and, while few would accept his Gothic description, 'On summer days the outlook was bright and even gladsome; but at sundown in September, with a high wind, and a heavy surf rolling in close along the links, the place told of nothing but dead mariners and sea disaster', it is an impressive sweep which sets off the view across the Firth of Forth to Fife, the cliffs of Elie and the two Lomonds. To the immediate west lie the yellow dunes guarding Gullane Bay, originally harmless but more recently the scene of coastal erosion on a scale that has needed thatching and planting by an enlightened County Council. Westward in the Firth lies the small island of Inchkeith and, on a clear day, the cantilevers of the Forth Rail Bridge and the pillars of the Road Bridge over twenty miles away are clearly visible – as are Arthur's Seat and the chimneys of Edinburgh. The view to the south embraces the Lammermuir Hills and the rich farm country of East Lothian. Pheasant, partridge and hare find the links a peaceful habitation, as though they realised that the knickerbockered sportsmen are not, as John Betjeman said, trudging 'in syndicated shoot'. The birds never move for a ball landing among them, but rise at once when a questing golfer approaches.

The ground in 1891, when the Honourable Company took possession, was completely virgin, more lush, and less sandy than on the other seaside links in East Lothian and at St. Andrews. This was a very unusual quality and there is no doubt that Andrew Kirkaldy's ill-tempered description of it was wide of the mark. But the great old St. Andrews professional had just seen the first Open Championship at Muirfield in 1892 won, not only by an amateur (Mr. H. H. Hilton), but by one from South Britain. His indignation was understandable.

In the 1890s the northern boundary was a stone wall which, although hidden sufficiently not to foreshorten the view from the Clubhouse, restricted the space available for the full length of eighteen holes. The confined nature of the new links became even more apparent when the gutta-percha ball was replaced in 1902 by the Haskell which flew much further and made inevitable some counter-measures by those in charge of courses.

The offending wall ran from Archerfield at a point near the present sixth green, excluding the seventh and thirteenth greens, and thence to the north-west corner of the course at the present third tee. Traces of its foundation are still apparent in the contours of the third fairway. The Honourable Company managed by stages to push out their northern boundary and to remove the wall. Other improvements were made in order to lengthen the course to championship standards, but it was not until the 1920s that the circuit settled down to its present form. Each time a major championship comes to Muirfield, new back tees are built and other minor alterations made – a development much regretted by older members who reluctantly concede that, although 'Medal tees' have little place in the Honourable Company's mystique, some stretching is needed when professionals appear for a lucrative contest before the television cameras. The longer tees, however, have been introduced so as to avoid interfering with the play of members throughout the year and the tees from which Medals are played have remained practically the same since 1926.

The Club Minutes of the period are strangely silent about the planning and construction of the new course in the years 1890–91, but the various earth-moving activities at Muirfield did not escape the vigilant eye of the Rev. John Kerr who, as a member and a *Scotsman* reporter, was present at the opening ceremony. He records that David Plenderleith put into effect the design staked out by Tom Morris, Senior, the greenkeeper from St. Andrews, who had won the Championship Belt four times, in 1861, 1862, 1864 and 1867, and was later to play in the first two Open Championships at Muirfield in 1892 and 1896. Plenderleith had as assistants, Robert Ross, Robert Brown, whose name, as a greenkeeper, appears in the Minutes, Fred Hamilton, who later acquired a great reputation as one of Muirfield's famous head greenkeepers, and Andrew Allan. These four 'dumped away with their iron beaters, levelled mounds, filled up rabbit scrapes, banked up bunkers, turfed, rolled and swept continuously'. For their energy, skill and devotion to their unusual task, we salute them.

On 2nd May, 1891, sixteen holes were opened for play and the remaining two were completed in time for the opening of the new Clubhouse in December of the same year. There is little about the original eighteen holes which would attract attention, critical or otherwise, now; but reports of the 1892 Open in the *Scotsman* were complimentary and spoke of the course as 'providing good golf, sporting shots, tricky but fair greens' and, last but not least, 'good fun'. But members of the Honourable Company always seem to have realised that there was room for improvement and, in 1894, an unthinkable event finally stirred the Committee to action. At the Spring Meeting, Mr. R. H. Johnston, the Recorder, won the Gold Medal with a score of 79; 48 out, and 31 for the inward half. A course that made this possible for 'quite an ordinary golfer' could not possibly be up to championship standards. Mr. Johnston's own view of this offensively realistic reaction is not known, but a remeasurement disclosed that the course was well under the requisite three miles. It was clear that something had to be done before the Open returned to Muirfield in 1896. Mr. R. H. Don Wauchope, a member with a great Scottish sporting name, produced a plan which lengthened the course by over 600 yards before the 1896 Open. It now measured 6,194 yards.

The 1906 Open Championship was the first at Muirfield after the Haskell ball came into general use and, once again, the course was found to be too short. Under much the same weather conditions as when he won in 1901, James Braid's winning aggregate was nine strokes fewer. The Honourable Company saw the reputation of their course at risk and decided to approach the owner of the Dirleton Estates to sell some more ground at the north-east corner of the course. As a result, the wall was moved northwards and alterations to the eighth, ninth and tenth holes were made which lengthened the course, while a further sprinkling of additional bunkers made it more difficult. It was on this course, as now extended, that the 1909 Amateur, 1912 Open, and 1920 Amateur Championships took place.

The first hole (204 yards) was a longish short hole from a tee near the end of the private road to the Clubhouse to a green not far from the boundary wall. For those disinclined to risk going out of bounds, the rough on the right was heavy and necessitated an uphill approach over bunkers to a tilted green with many borrows. Just the right hole for the members to work off the lunch-time brandy.

The Second hole (365 yards) went from a tee close to the boundary wall, almost due west. Its feature was a semi-circular bunker guarding the green which caught a drive or a second, according to the prowess of the striker and the direction of the wind, which is generally from the west. The rough on the right, as all over the course, was adhesive and uninviting.

The third hole (336 yards) was almost exactly the same as the present second. If there were not so many bunkers on the right, the marshy hollow on the left was even more menacing. Here, many years later, Joe Carr was to win a controversial extra-holes tie against the Tasmanian champion, Toogood, in the Amateur Championship. Carr claimed that the wet grass on the left constituted casual water; was upheld by a Royal and Ancient representative hurriedly extracted from the Clubhouse; lifted, dropped and, to rub salt in the wounds, got a birdie three to dismiss a very discomfited opponent.

The fourth hole (347 yards) turned more to the south-east than the present third. Its main feature was a hollow, out of which the approach had to be played over a sleeper-faced bunker of formidable size, to a blind green which, as it also served as the fourteenth green, was large, and a putt of over 30 yards was not uncommon.

The fifth hole (470 yards) continued east and favoured those of strong nerves for whom the bunker escarpment facing the tee had no terrors.

The sixth hole had two tees; one, a championship tee, which was north of the fifth green and extended the hole to 383 yards. Once again, the tee shot towards the south favoured the strong who, by faith more than sight, played at the bunker-top facing them and were duly rewarded by an easier second. Throughout the hole the green wooden windmill dominated the scene, although it never came into the line of play. This bizarre structure had been erected over a natural well when the Honourable Company first came to Muirfield and, at first, provided the water supply for the Clubhouse. The windmill was blown down in 1920, but the well is still used as a reinforcement in times of drought for watering the greens. It is concealed amidst the bushes just to the north of the practice ground tee (and can also be reached by a quick slice from the present tenth tee).

The *seventh hole* continued along the Archerfield Wall to near the present eighth green. It was well bunkered and the best line was to the right and thence over the cross bunkers, which were placed almost as they are now for the eighth.

The *eighth hole* (497 yards off championship tee; 472 off medal tee) was not unlike the present ninth, but the rough beyond the present left-hand bunker from the tee was a mixture of scrubby, sandy bents and a bunker sleepered in parts.

The *ninth hole* (365 yards), a dog leg to the right, came back to a green which is now the south-east corner of the practice ground. Short, and slightly to the right of the green, was a pond where there was an implement thoughtfully provided to retrieve errant balls.

The *tenth hole* (390 yards) went north-westwards and, it must be admitted, lacked distinction.

The *eleventh hole* (407 yards) turned back towards the Clubhouse and was marked by two sets of cross bunkers to catch the tee shot and the duffed second. In those days, cross bunkers were much in favour, and the dreadful effectiveness of the few that remain at Muirfield – the eighth, tenth, fifteenth and seventeenth come readily to mind – suggest that they are still the most punishing type of hazard, even with modern equipment.

The *twelfth hole* (390 yards) went almost due north from about the present forward tenth tee, its great feature being the second shot across the biggest bunker on the course (part of the present seventeenth green) to a slightly raised plateau green.

The remaining six holes now followed the old 1896 course.

The *thirteenth hole* (293 yards) turned slightly south-westward and was best played as a dog-leg, approaching the green from the left.

The fourteenth hole (138 yards) was the only really short hole. From a slightly raised tee, the player faced a naturally eroded lower level of rough, wispy, scrubby ground ending in a bunker proper, above which rose a partly sleepered escarpment. On the reverse slope, part of the green was blind. It may not have been an ideal short hole but it was one of the few which raised legitimate hopes of entering at least one three on the card.

The fifteenth hole (295 yards off championship tee), which stretched towards the north-west corner of the course, had a cross bunker to negotiate from the tee, and the same convex or herring-bone shaped green as at present.

The sixteenth hole (464 yards) pointed south-east towards the Clubhouse. Starting with a forbidding carry over jungly rough, now discernible to the right front of the present sixteenth tee, it then followed a rig and furrow type of fairway (also still in existence from the present seventeenth tee) to a cross bunker, which only a long hitter could carry in two, to a well guarded green. It was a slog; a rather dull hole with little prospect of satisfactory accomplishment.

The seventeenth hole (330 yards) turned northwards again. Slightly dog-legged, to the left there was plenty of trouble for those who tried to cut the corner.

The eighteenth hole (382 yards) offered a fine finish, even if it did not equal the magnificence of its present successor. Its most memorable features were cross bunkers to be carried both from the tee and with the second shot if a four was to be achieved. Early photographs show repellent sleepers in the faces of the bunkers guarding the green. It was not a difficult hole, but it was made no easier by the unnerving expectation that there would be watchers in the Clubhouse, as nowadays, wagering on the likelihood of some atrocity, such as the head up or, perhaps, the shank.

1919 saw some significant technical changes in the layout of the course which were completed in time for the Amateur Championship played in the following year. For those who retain a cartographic interest in the evolution of the links, the main alteration was the construction of a new seventh, on the lines of the present hole, measuring 170 yards, but with bunkers beyond the green as well as on the flanks. The eighth, measuring 465 yards, was not unlike the present hole except that, instead of bushes and bunkers on the right, there was only rough. At the ninth the ground which lay beyond the bunker on the left was a mixture of scrub and bunkers and there was no clandestine, punitive bunker in the centre of the fairway some 40 yards from the green, as there is now. The old Pond Hole remained, but as the tenth, instead of the ninth; and the course followed on the same old lines until the thirteenth, which now went due north and measured 390 yards. It had cross bunkers to negotiate from the tee and was slightly dog-leg to the left to avoid a clutch of eight fearsome bunkers in series. The fourteenth was the old thirteenth, and the old short fourteenth was no more. Instead, the sequence was now straight to the former fifteenth, and thence, by the old route, home. The course measured 6,501 yards, compared with 6,328 in 1912.

In spite of these changes, which represented a very sensible piece of tidying up, the course was still too cramped within the constricting wall which still existed, except in the north-east corner. At last, in 1922, after much negotiation the Honourable Company's original shortsightedness was put right. An additional 50 acres of land in the north was purchased and plans for what amounted to a new course were produced by the English golf course architect, Mr. Harry Colt, relying for local advice mainly on Mr. Robert Maxwell. The new layout was completed in 1925 and in the following year the changes met with general approval during the Amateur Championship.

Inevitably, there have been changes since 1926, with a view to adding to the intriguing nature of individual holes and making the course more testing. It is also necessary to allow ever-increasing space for spectators, television cameras, trade exhibitions and so on, at major tournaments. But the Honourable Company have never lost sight of the need to preserve the course primarily for the use and enjoyment of the members and the average golfer. New hazards have been created and back tees constructed to stretch the sinews of the gladiators in the championships, but members have (thankfully) never been called upon to use them.

The general layout of the new course is simple. It winds like a giant intestine. The first nine holes lie in a clockwise circuit round the outer boundary of the course and end at the ninth, a hundred yards to the east of the Clubhouse. The second nine run counter-clockwise, inside the first nine, with the result that the player finds the wind coming at him from every angle during the progress of his round. There is no question, as at St. Andrews or Troon, of fighting continuously against the wind on the outward half and then coasting home with it, or *vice versa*. At Muirfield the wind does not come from the same direction for more than three holes consecutively. And wind there is. A true Muirfield man has been known to complain that, on calm days, he finds it difficult to maintain his balance 'for lack of something to lean against'.

Of the changes since 1926, the most important has been the alteration of the short thirteenth hole. Initially, the green was hard up against the bank to the right of the present one. It was long and narrow, sloping down from rear to front, with a particularly steep slope dividing the green into an upper and lower layer. At the lower end of the green was a cross bunker into which it was demonstrably possible to putt from the top half when the ground was fast and the wind following. Both sides of the narrow green were heavily bunkered. As a hole it was great fun and a good tee shot was well rewarded, but luck saved the bad shot often enough to seem inequitable, and so the hole was altered to its present form, and the remains of the old hole have completely disappeared.

At the first hole, originally there was a string of bunkers along nearly the whole length of the right side of the fairway. They remained until it was realised that bunkers require much expensive and time-consuming maintenance and that rough is often a more punishing hazard. Indeed, in 1928 there were about 225 bunkers on the course (never 365, as is often stated), compared with 170 in 1970.

Another permanent feature was added at the eighth hole. This is a dog-leg hole, and the hazards on the right, designed to prevent cutting the corner, were bunkers and rough. During the Open Championship in 1929, the crowd trampled down the rough and enabled the ultimate winner, Walter Hagen, to aim purposely out to the right. To prevent this contemptuous feat being repeated, a thick clump of buckthorn and other bushes was planted. Many subsequent golfers, who have been trapped in the petrified forest, have remembered Hagen's ingenuity without any great sense of gratitude.

At the ninth, a new bunker has been dug in the middle of the fairway some 40 yards from the green, 20 yards from the boundary wall, and less from the bunkers on the right. It is the only wholly blind bunker on the course which cannot be predicted by the unknowing. It is known as 'Simpson's Folly' after the golf architect who suggested it.

In 1966 the course measured 6,887 yards. In order to make mad the guilty and appal the free at the Open Championship of 1972, new back tees at the fifth, eleventh, seventeenth and eighteenth will make it well over 7,000 yards, as follows:

The first hole (456 yards) starts from just below the roundabout at the end of the road to the Clubhouse and proceeds westwards towards Gullane Hill, more often than not against the prevailing wind. It is a searching par 4. The drive has to be directed onto a fairway which, at its narrowest, measures under 20 yards, with a bunker on the left and typical tenacious Muirfield rough on the right. The nearer to the left of the fairway, the easier the second to a well-trapped green with a narrow entry on the left. Only with experience is it realised that the green slopes away from the front to the back. An optical illusion makes this hard to detect.

The second hole (359 yards), the sole survivor of the 1891 course (it was the old third), heads towards the Firth of Forth. It is an innocent enough looking hole and, while the drive ought not to present much difficulty, the second shot has to go between the encroaching Gullane dunes held back by the wall and wattled fencing on the left and a honeycomb of bunkers on the right. The green is both hard, with a rocky foundation, and difficult to read. Those who survived till the last day of the 1966 Open averaged over the par 4 for this hole: sure evidence of its exacting nature.

The third hole (388 yards) heads straight east and requires an accurately placed drive to allow entry through the spines of two hillocks, each decorated with a cavernous bunker ready for the mistimed shot.

The fourth hole (189 yards) is a testing short hole; a long carry to the plateau-shaped front of the green; severe bunkers for the half-hit tee-shot; and precipitous borrows on the green. A par is exceptionally welcome.

The fifth hole (572 yards) continues east along the northern edge of the course. There is an inspiring view of ships on the Firth and the distant prospect of the Fife coast. This is invariably a punishing hole. For the average golfer it usually means a lot of golf. For the 1972 Open the tee will have been taken a further 40 yards to a lonely site right in the buck-thorn, and the hole will impose a severe examination for even the longest hitters.

The sixth hole (450 yards) turns south and brings the Lammermuirs into direct vision. It has a special championship tee some 150 yards nearer Archerfield Woods, which makes it as sharp a dog-leg to the left as is to be found anywhere. To cut the corner often spells disaster as, apart from bunkers, the rough is of the thickest, and a compass is needed to find the way out. A shot to the right opens up the green in the distance near

Archerfield Wood. Here, hares are often put up, and fir cones carried by birds from the woods will be found on the fairway.

The seventh hole (194 yards), like the sixth, has a special championship tee some 25 yards further back than the normal one. The green is an elevated one, exposed to winds from all directions. Overshooting carries heavy penalties in impervious rough. To complete the unusual difficulties, few players can be convinced, or convince themselves, that nearly all putts on the green are straight. Overborrowing is almost inevitable.

The eighth hole (445 yards) often requires two full shots to clear the repelling bastion of cross bunkers. A par 4 is invariably a source of thankfulness.

The ninth hole (498 yards) is regarded by many leading authorities as the best, as well as the most difficult, on the course. Jack Nicklaus, when winning the 1966 Open, never attempted to reach the green in two and was content with a par 5 in each round. Throughout the hole, the hazards lie at an angle across the line of flight. A long tee shot has to be steered through a narrow neck of fairway between a bunker and rough, and against a strong west wind it is only from there that the green can be reached in two. For the second shot, there is out of bounds to the left; Simpson's Folly (already described); and a number of bunkers in echelon on the right. The green slopes from left to right and there is no banking to prevent overrunning.

The tenth hole (475 yards) starts the inner circuit and goes due north. From a tee almost in the garden of Greywalls Hotel, the drive has to be steered to the left of the fairway to avoid two cunningly placed bunkers on the right, celebrated for their magnetic attraction. Two cross bunkers, which appear to await the second shot with an air of unshakeable confidence, lie ahead. The second shot is partly blind with two more infuriating bunkers on the right front of the green – which itself contains as many hidden borrows as any. For the sadistic spectator, this is as good a place as any to watch the ritual of 2–3 ft. putts being missed.

The eleventh hole (378 yards) continues northwards and is characterised by the only blind drive on the course. The line is to the left of the guidepost on the cross ridge, and is dictated by a bunker on the right and often, too, by the flag being tucked in behind further bunkers on the right. The green is also trapped to the left and also maliciously behind; an unusual feature at Muirfield.

With *the twelfth hole* (390 yards) there is an unmistakable sense of turning for home and realising that only a few opportunities remain to master the adversary. Against a west wind, the second shot to an elongated green, sloping from left to right and guarded by bunkers along both sides, is a glorious one and has to be boldly struck. With an east wind, especially when the ground is hard, it is difficult to stop on the green from any distance.

The thirteenth hole (163 yards) goes eastwards uphill to an elusive, fast, long and narrow green cradled amongst hillocks and guarded by deep, satanic bunkers from which it is often neither possible nor wise to recover direct towards the hole. It was here, in 1948, with King George VI as an appreciative spectator, that C. H. Ward holed his tee shot.

The fourteenth hole (456 yards) is slightly dog-legged to the left, and the line from the tee is as near the cluster of bunkers on the left as possible, there being a small, but dangerously enticing, trap on the right. The green has a fiendish borrow from all angles.

The fifteenth hole (403 yards) presents few problems off the tee for a good player but, with a plague of cross bunkers to negotiate, the average hitter often has the humiliating experience of trying to gauge how far to the left he dare go and still achieve the carry. The green, known as the Camel's Back and shaped like a herring bone, speaks for itself, and its message is always a convex one. This green has been in existence since the first course was constructed.

The sixteenth hole (197 yards) faces south-east towards the Clubhouse and is an exacting 3. The ground, in particular the dip in front of the green, makes the choice of club important, especially as the green has a steep bank rising from front to back, and many a too timid shot can land on the green and then roll back some yards, sometimes even into a bunker judiciously placed on the left. Once again a bold tee shot is required, even although the putt downhill, when the ground is hard, can be a nightmare.

The seventeenth hole (571 yards), which is to be lengthened in 1972 by some 50 yards by pushing the tee further back, features bunkers and rough on the left for those who impertinently try to cut the dog-leg too much in order to secure a reasonable shot to the green. There remain four cross bunkers, two of such depth that one visitor enquired whether they had been built as lion cages or elephant traps. No visit to Muirfield is complete till extraction from these formidable caverns has been essayed.

The eighteenth hole (445 yards) provides a suitable grandstand finish over the diamond-shaped complex of bunkers towards the Clubhouse. Here, Gary Player took 6 at the end of his victorious bid for the 1959 Open, and Henry Cotton took a 5 in his winning year, having played two from a greenside bunker and holing a heroic putt to do so. Just where a good tee shot lands, lie three extensive traps on the left, looking across to a sizeable colleague on the right. The green is heavily fortified with bunkers, the one on the right, with its grass island in the middle, being as difficult as the diabolical one on the left.

Muirfield enjoys the happiest of climates. Rainstorms from the west are bisected by Gullane Hill; half go south-east along the Lammermuir Hills, while the other half disappear down the Firth. There is little frost or snow, and few interruptions with the serious business of club matches throughout the year. For example, in the winter months of 1970/71 there was not a single day when play was made impossible because of snow, frost or rain. Because of the sandy soil, the quick drainage and the condition of the rough, the course throughout the winter months is thought by many to be in its best and most enjoyable condition. The green staff are unceasingly active, and many visitors have commented on the excellence of the work of James Logan, head greenkeeper for twenty-two years, and his assistants – worthy successors to Fred Hamilton, James Torley and other experts of the past.

CHAPTER VI

BAY LEAVES (I) (1892–1912)

Muirfield is a championship course and it has been on the rota since 1892. The Honourable Company realise that the improvements to the course made over the years, and the memories of great championships played there, combine to make the links at Muirfield a national asset and that they are the custodians. Accordingly, every few years they welcome visitors to watch the leading gladiators of the day in combat. Many of the most celebrated professionals have often said that they regard Muirfield as the fairest test of all and that they would as soon win the Open Championship there as on any other course. This may be because they share Bernard Darwin's view that 'There is a jolly view of the sea and rather a fascinating wood, with its trees all bent and twisted by the wind, and, which is more to the point, some uncommonly difficult golf to be played'. But there are very likely other more pertinent reasons. For example, professionals greatly dislike blind shots which import an awkward element of unpredictable chance, and the only blind shot at Muirfield is the drive at the eleventh. The professionals also reckon that, while the links have been lengthened for successive championships, it is not really a slogger's course and length by itself will not prevail. The bunkers, though enormous and chasm-like, are reckoned to provide fair hazards. They are not capriciously or unfairly sited and are designed to catch only the less than true shot. It must be admitted, however, that the professionals' comments on the texture and height of the rough have been known to be much less complimentary.

Throughout the year the course is kept in order for the enjoyment of the members and their guests but, despite its carefully preserved anonymity and despite the absence of numbered indicators, distances or individual names for the holes, the ghosts of past champions will linger over the Hundred Acre field and import their own personality. Robert Maxwell, invincible when he won his two championships there; the then unknown Harry Vardon, winning the second Open Championship at Muirfield;

James Braid's first success: all these are freshly remembered. So, too, are the genial impertinence of Walter Hagen cutting the corner at the eighth; Alf Perry, an unexpected, but worthy, winner, striding home with two courageous wooden shots to each of the last two greens; Henry Cotton, lingering for what seemed an interminable time in the last bunker; and, most recently of all, the stands rising to Jack Nicklaus as he marched down the eighteenth fairway on his final round to claim his championship. No one can play round Muirfield without having pointed out to him where some hero of the past hit a god-like shot to the pin or, perhaps, shanked under pressure.

For those who do not come to play at Muirfield, it is a name which comes to notice only on the occasion of these national and international events. It is a course to be indentified from press accounts or, more recently, to be seen on the television screen to the accompaniment of the erudite comments of Mr. Henry Longhurst, surely the most mellifluous and informed of commentators. The championships are, accordingly, a more integral part of the history of the Honourable Company than might appear at first sight, and it is for this reason that they are described in these chapters – a description which will attempt no dry statistical analysis, but will seek to elicit some of the flavour of the recurring events.

The real credit for starting both the Amateur and Open Championships can rightly be claimed by the Prestwick Golf Club. Until then there had been domestic competitions run by various clubs and societies, and there had been many exciting challenge matches undertaken by the growing band of professionals, particularly during the middle of last century when Alan Robertson, the Morrises, the Dunns and the Parks played for what were then quite high stakes of £200 or more. But these were not really organised events which would justify the winner's claiming the title of champion. On 6th April, 1857, Prestwick wrote to a number of clubs inviting them to 'send four members to contend: the game to be played in Doubles or Foursomes drawing for opponents by lot before starting and again after each game by the winners, the remaining winning pair to be considered Champions. The Prizes for the competition to be a Medal, or other piece of Plate purchased at the expense of the competing Clubs in proportion to the number of members in each. At the conclusion of the playing by pairs, the winning pair will compete in a single match for the prize in a single match, the winner to become the Possessor.' This letter seems to have been sent originally to the clubs at St. Andrews, Perth,

ROBERT MAXWELL
Captain 1912 and 1913

Musselburgh, Blackheath, Carnoustie, North Berwick and Leven. It aroused an immediate and enthusiastic response and five other clubs (the Honourable Company, the Royal Burgess Society, Bruntsfield Links, Montrose and Dirleton) said that they did not wish to be left out. By the time the tournament took place in July 1857, and by general consent it was held at St. Andrews, the number of representatives from each club had been reduced to a single foursome pair. For reasons which are not now evident, neither the Honourable Company nor the Panmure Club of Carnoustie fielded a team; and the final was won by Royal Blackheath represented by Mr. George Glennie and Lt. J. C. Stewart who beat the Royal and Ancient by seven holes.

It was soon felt that a competition where the winning foursome pair were then required to compete with each other was not a satisfactory formula. This had an unwelcome air of fratricide and so, for the second championship in 1858, an individual contest was introduced. There was an entry of twenty-eight, and the competition followed much the same lines as the present Amateur Championship. By a strange coincidence, which would have commended itself to an epic poet, the final was played between the youngest competitor, Robert Chambers from the publishing firm, aged twenty, who had entered from the Bruntsfield Links Society, and D. Wallace of Leven who was over sixty and much the oldest player in the field. Under the rules (still followed in some of the Royal and Ancient and other competitions) both players in a halved match proceeded to the next round neither having been eliminated and, ironically, Chambers and Wallace had already halved twice before they met in the final. Even in those days, slow play was a source of irritation, and it was recorded that Wallace, who was notoriously languid, 'would have carried the championship at the Final tussle by his wearisome style, had not Robert Chambers' temper been particularly easy going'. Chambers is reported as saying: 'Give me a novel and a camp-stool and I'll let the old chap do as he likes'. Robert Chambers triumphed by a single hole. The set of silver plate which he won was presented to the Honourable Company on his death by his son and is still preserved at Muirfield along with the set of clubs won by the runner-up.

It could reasonably be argued that the Prestwick Club had, by now, established the Amateur Championship, although formal recognition was not to come for some time, and they now turned their attention to starting a similar event which would also be open to professionals. The

F

Open Championship, as it is now known, was started by the Prestwick Club in 1860 and played over their course until 1870. As a trophy for the winner, the Club presented a champion's belt to be held for a year. Their generosity, perhaps on the assumption that they would never be called to account, extended to prescribing that anyone who won the belt for three successive years would be entitled to retain it as his own property. Tom Morris, Jnr., however, achieved this feat in 1870. No championship was held in 1871, but in 1872 a new trophy, in the shape of the present cup, was subscribed for by Prestwick, the Royal and Ancient and the Honourable Company, and the championship was played in successive years over the links of these clubs until 1893.

The 1892 championship, the first to be held at Muirfield, has already been briefly described in the chapter on the Muirfield Green. Bernard Darwin's conclusion was that Muirfield was a course 'of good omen for amateurs, for the first championship that was played on it – in 1892 – certainly showed the amateurs in a brighter light than any other championship since. At the end of the first two rounds, Mr. Horace Hutchinson was the leader; at the end of the third, Mr. Ball led, with Mr. Hilton second; and at the end of the fourth, Mr. Hilton was open champion, and Mr. Ball, if I remember aright, tied for second place.' And, he concluded ruefully, 'I am afraid we shall never live to see such another championship as that'.

An objective record must mention that, when the Honourable Company moved from Musselburgh in 1891, the inclusion of Muirfield in the championship rota did not meet with universal acceptance throughout the golfing world. First, there was the drawback of its inaccessibility; then it was demonstrably a very new course; it was confined by a wall which greatly restricted its length, even in the days of the gutty; and there were many critics who claimed that it was not nearly severe enough a test. Some support for this view could be found from the figures. The winning score in the 1892 Open had been 305. During the next three years when the championship was held at Prestwick, Sandwich and St. Andrews, the winning aggregate had been 322, 326 and 322 respectively. Something had to be done if Muirfield, like the other championship courses, was still to be able to separate the men from the boys; and, for the 1896 Open Championship, the course had been lengthened by 600 yards. Strenuous efforts were made by the Green Committee to improve its condition and it was said to be six or seven strokes more difficult. *The Times* condescended to say that nothing but praise was heard regarding the links, and added, in Jove-like fashion, that 'a difference of opinion will always exist as to the relative merits of the first class courses in the Kingdom but few will deny that Muirfield possesses all the characteristics of a Championship green'.

The 1896 championship is perhaps best remembered as providing the first triumph for Harry Vardon: but he was not the favourite and, for most of the play, it did not look as though he would win. After the first thirty-six holes, J. H. Taylor, with rounds of 77 and 78, was a stroke ahead of his great rival, Alex Herd, who had, however, stolen the lime-light with a first round of 72. Contemporary reports thought it doubtful whether such a feat had ever before been accomplished in golfing history and, if we are to believe press accounts, 'driving a long ball he pitched in most deadly fashion and over and over again holed from his approach'. But no man can continue on this supernatural plane and, on his second round, Herd fell somewhat from his lofty eminence and was a stroke behind Taylor at half way. At this stage, Mr. Freddie Tait upheld the amateur cause by lying third.

The second and last day's play produced perfect weather and, for the first time at Muirfield, a very large crowd appeared, many having taken the train to Drem and then walked the three and a half miles to the course. But none of them seemed to have realised that Vardon was a possible winner. Partnered by Mr. H. H. Hilton, he played part of his last round without a single spectator following him, and only ten people saw his last shot. Beforehand, at the end of the third round, Herd was a stroke ahead of Taylor, with Vardon three more behind. Herd collapsed in the afternoon, and Taylor and Vardon, with 80 and 77 respectively, tied for the lead with only Mr. Tait out on the course with any chance of catching them. He needed a 74 to win and, with six holes to play (including the one really short hole on the course), he needed only level fours. A 3 at the short fourteenth and a 4 at the fifteenth kept him in the running, and prospects of another Scottish triumph began to appear on the horizon. But it proved too much for him and he finished 6, 5, 5, to tie for third place with Willie Fernie from Dumfries. In the re-play over thirty-six holes, Vardon won his first crown by four strokes (78 plus 79 against 80 plus 81 by Taylor). The total prize money for the 1896 championship amounted to £100. Vardon's win was also significant as marking the triumph of a professional stylist, and his grip and swing long served as a model.

1897 saw the Amateur Championship staged at Muirfield for the first time since its inception in 1885. In the intervening years, the championship had been largely monopolised by a quintet of great amateur golfers who towered above their contemporaries – H. G. Hutchinson, John Ball, Freddie Tait, L. M. Balfour-Melville and J. E. Laidlay. The last three were Scots, and the last two distinguished members of the Honourable Company. In 1897, however, the form was faulted very early and only one of the five Corinthians, Balfour-Melville, reached the last eight, where he was defeated by the eventual winner, A. J. T. Allan of Edinburgh University. This was a year when youth was both on the prow and at the helm, for Allan was only twenty-one and his defeated opponent in the final – from a record entry of seventy-four – was a nineteen-year-old student from St. Andrews, James Robb.

Allan is one of the most intriguing figures in the history of golf. At the time of his victory, he was a medical student at Edinburgh University, and he had taken up golf only six years previously on the Braid Hills course, a public links on the outskirts of the town. Another unusual aspect of his success also attracted a great deal of attention at the time. During each day of the championship, he travelled by train from Edinburgh to Drem and then by bicycle to Muirfield, returning each evening by the same means. To complete his nonchalant attitude to the normal requirements of the game, he played golf in the same shoes in which he had travelled from Edinburgh, and they had neither studs nor spikes. He was of slight physique, and those who saw him play commented on his graceful and easy swing. He won 'with wonderful coolness for so young a hand'. Unfortunately, he died before the next year's championship, and it may well be that his true potential was never realised. His memory is appropriately commemorated by the 'Jack Allan Cup' which is played for annually by the Scottish Universities.

His defeated opponent, James Robb, was runner-up again in 1900 when H. H. Hilton won, but, on his third final in 1906 at Hoylake, he had a richly deserved victory. He played for Scotland against England five times from 1902 onwards. But, good player though Robb undoubtedly was, and better though he proved to be, there is no doubt that 1897 was Allan's year and all others were eclipsed.

Until 1920, the Open Championship was staged, managed and generally administered in turn by the seven clubs over whose links it was played. The seven in question were Prestwick, the Royal and Ancient and the

Honourable Company; Royal Liverpool (Hoylake) and Royal St. Georges (Sandwich), who had been added to the championship rota in 1893; and Royal Cinque Ports (Deal) and the Troon Club, who were included in 1909. The club where the championship was played had to undertake all the arrangements for that particular year, including advertising the dates, attracting entries, providing facilities for spectators and the press and, a growing problem, marshalling the spectators. The problems were, however, still pretty minimal by present-day standards. It was sufficient to pitch a marquee in order to provide suitable accommodation for victualling and drinking. At Muirfield in 1901, we are told that the press were well looked after by the Clubmaster's wife, Mrs. Pinner, and the spectators, who at that time tended to be enthusiasts, well-versed in the game and behaviour on the course, gave very little trouble. But, as a sign of things to come, the 1901 championship saw as many as 4,000 people watching play on a single day.

At the start of the 1901 championship, *The Times* announced that –

> The Competition for the greatest honour in golf was begun yesterday under the direction of the Honourable Company of Edinburgh Golfers at Muirfield. The arrangements for the meeting are under the superintendence of Mr. H. Patten, W.S., Secretary of the Honourable Company [of whom we have already heard] . . . The course is almost at its best but perhaps the putting greens are a trifle keen. To add to the difficulties, the players had to cope with a strong westerly breeze.

This was James Braid's year. There was a record entry of 101 (19 amateurs) and thirty-six holes were played on each of the two days. For the first time a guillotine was applied for the final day and the odd rule was that, provided a minimum of thirty-two professionals were allowed to qualify, only those less than twenty strokes behind the leader were to be eligible to play the last two rounds. In the event, two amateurs from the Honourable Company succeeded in qualifying for the last day. At the end of the first day's play, Vardon and Braid tied for the lead at 155, with J. H. Taylor (the holder) at 162. The battle was really among these three and, eventually, Braid won with an aggregate of 309; Vardon was runner-up three strokes behind; and Taylor one stroke behind him. This was the first of Braid's five wins in the Open Championship and was, naturally, extremely popular with the predominantly Scottish gallery. A contemporary report said that it was 'a splendid victory for a great golfer. Braid has long been a fine golfer through the green, but this time

his putting did not desert him as it had been wont to do in the past.'
He celebrated his triumph by christening his second son 'Harry Muirfield'.

Two years later, in 1903, the Amateur Championship returned to
Muirfield and, for the first time in the history of the tournament, the large
entry (142, including seventy-nine Scots and sixty English players) made
it necessary to extend play over four days. The clutch of famous ex-
champions – Hutchinson, Ball, Hilton, Balfour-Melville and Laidlay –
was again in the field, though none of them was to succeed. Before the
championship, the second amateur international between Scotland and
England took place with England getting their revenge for their 1902
defeat by five matches to four. In the championship itself, England and
Scotland each had four players in the last eight; the excitement was
intense, and the play attracted many spectators. Much to the satisfaction
of the home crowd, Robert Maxwell, entered on this occasion from the
local Tantallon Golf Club, was the ultimate winner. At this time he was
twenty-six years old, but he had already made his reputation in the golfing
world. In the 1897 Amateur Championship at Muirfield he had leapt into
prominence by beating John Ball and H. H. Hilton, and in 1902 he was
the leading amateur in the Open Championship. On this occasion he
marched steadily through the early rounds. The unfortunate S. A. Gillon,
who had already overcome several notable players, fell, in the words of
Horace Hutchinson, 'into the hands of Mr. Maxwell and was flogged
unmercifully'. In the semi-final, however, Maxwell was hard pressed by
H. W. de Zoete of Royal St. Georges, whom he beat only at the nineteenth by negotiating a stymie. In the final he was in rampant form and
poor Hutchinson fared no better than Gillon and was beaten by seven and
five. Bernard Darwin said that Maxwell was just a little bit better at
Muirfield than anywhere else and that he gauged the length of deceptive
iron shots with an ease born of much practice and was able to putt on the
Muirfield greens 'which is more than many people can do'.

1906 saw the Open back at Muirfield. The large entry was increased
by one when Sandy Herd (the holder), on arriving to defend his title,
found that his entry had not been received. Delays in the post were not
such a recent innovation as might be supposed nowadays, and the
Committee of the Honourable Company were characteristically merciful
and allowed Herd to play.

This was the first major tournament at Muirfield in which the new
Haskell ball was generally used, and its better flight was such an improve-

ment that no doubt was left that the course would have to be lengthened and made more exacting. The winning aggregate in this year, under very similar conditions, was nine strokes better than in 1901 when the gutta-percha ball was still in use. Indeed, ever since the opening of the century there had been a continual struggle between skills and improved equipment and the length and difficulty of the championship courses. The gutty flew far, but low, and the shape of courses had been altered accordingly with a plague of clumsy, frontal hazards, but the rubber-cored Haskell could easily be lofted over an opposing dyke or mound, and so, from 1903 onwards, the defences of the green were deployed in depth, with more skill and less like George II's infantry.

A further point on arms and ammunition is the oddity that, despite the efforts of skilled armourers like Sayers, Forgan and Nicoll, clubs have altered much less than balls. Fashions in woods changed, leaving persimmon for heads and hickory for shafts as the final choice before the introduction of steel shafts in 1929. But clubs of incredible antiquity still give satisfactory results. There have been freakish weapons, such as implements for playing round trees, and (now illegal) putters like croquet mallets, but it is clear from a comparison of wooden clubs with the venerable ones preserved in the dining-room at Muirfield that real changes have been few, and the infallible club remains the ultimate illusion.

By way of statistical leaven, the average score per round of the winner of the Open Championship between 1891 and 1901 was 78.5; between 1902 and 1926, it was 75.1; and from 1927 to 1949, it was 72.2. Since then, with every championship, new back tees are built, fairways are made narrower and the rough more ferocious. A championship course nowadays will be over 7,000 yards long, but the players are still on the ascendant and there have been occasions when an average of 70 has not been good enough to win: although, at Muirfield, an average of 71 has not been bettered to date.

To return to 1906: James Braid repeated his 1901 success at Muirfield with a contemptuous aggregate of 300 against 309 in the earlier championship. J. H. Taylor and Harry Vardon were again second and third, with 304 and 305 respectively, and an amateur, Mr. John Graham, Jnr., of Royal Liverpool, was fourth. Mr. Graham, a Scot who had learned his golf at Hoylake, was a player who commanded much respect but was to join the unhappy band of wandering spirits who had the ability but yet never succeeded in winning a champion's crown. Mr. Maxwell did well until the last round when he took 83 for an aggregate of 311.

The Times in early May 1909 carried a notice to would-be competitors that the Amateur Championhip would take place at Muirfield during the week beginning 24th May. The entry fee was one guinea and the value of the challenge cup, first played for in 1886, was stated to be £100. Lessons had been learned from the 1906 Open, and the course now set a much more searching examination. The first hole was moved to the right to make it a more difficult three; an extensive area of ground had been acquired at the north-east end and the wall at the back of the eighth and ninth greens had disappeared; some new diabolical bunkers had been dug, and the length now measured 6,230 yards. In the International preceding the championship, Scotland won by seven matches to two, the outstanding feature being Robert Maxwell's annihilation of John Ball by twelve and ten. This was his biggest win over Ball, but over the years when they met in these matches, usually leading their sides, Maxwell had the better cumulative record, winning five matches to Ball's two successes.

The last eight included four members of the Honourable Company – Robert Maxwell, J. E. Laidlay, N. F. Hunter and Captain C. K. Hutchinson. In the semi-final, Maxwell beat Bernard Darwin with an unbeatable round of 65 for the sixteen holes played. Most spectators thought that Maxwell could not be overcome and few foresaw how hard he would have to struggle to beat Captain Hutchinson on the last green in the final. Hutchinson was actually one up with two to play and came within a whisker of winning. Appreciative reports at the time said that there had never been such fine golf in a final of the Amateur; that it was improbable that there would be again for some time; and that both players deserved a gold medal. The play was described as nearly faultless and the speed of play and the friendly demeanour of the players entirely so. In the amicable atmosphere which they engendered, it was difficult to realise that a major championship was being decided. To one eye-witness, the most lasting impression was of Maxwell, totally unmoved, playing the last two holes. He dropped his right shoulder to a marked extent and used a very short back swing even for a full shot. The length came from a forceful turn of the body rather than from movement of the wrists; in short, a highly effective pivot.

There was to be one more Open, in 1912, before a grimmer contest superseded golf competitions. This one saw the introduction for the first time of qualifying rounds, and it was done in a pretty cumbrous way.

The field was divided into three sections with each playing thirty-six holes on one day at Muirfield during the week before the championship proper. The first twenty in each section were to qualify, and there were no exemptions. This was a long, drawn-out, painful business for spectators and players alike, especially for the players who qualified on the Thursday and had to wait the best part of a week, until the following Wednesday, before the championship was completed. Qualifying rounds remain a feature of the Open, but this unwieldy system was not repeated.

Bernard Darwin, already the most honoured of golfing correspondents, contemplating the forthcoming Open Championship, was still sceptical about the merits of Muirfield Green:

> It is now twenty years since Mr. Hilton won the first championship played at Muirfield; but there is still some suspicion of undue youthfulness attaching to the course. Perhaps because the course really was rather too new when the championship was first moved there, and because, moreover, there were many regrets for the glory which thereupon departed from Musselburgh, Muirfield has never quite got over that suspicion, once just, but now unjust.

After surveying the possible field, Bernard Darwin saw Braid as the most probable winner, with Vardon as the likely challenger, and prophesied that four 75s would be quite enough. He was wrong on both counts.

The main features of the qualifying rounds were two splendid scores of 70 and 73 by George Duncan, achieved in a north-west gale, which gave him a seven stroke lead in his section, and the failures of Robert Maxwell, possibly over-burdened with his duties as Captain of the Honourable Company, and of J. J. McDermott, the American Open champion. It was McDermott's unhappy fate to exemplify anew the maxim of La Rochefoucauld that we all have sufficient fortitude to bear other people's misfortunes; the sadistic pleasure of confirming their fallibility. At the seventh hole, a friendly crowd watched with compassion as he fired three drives in succession out of bounds into Archerfield Wood and was only saved from a fourth disaster by a rebound into the course from the intervening wall.

In the championship proper, Ted Ray of Oxhey won with four impressive rounds of 71, 73, 76 and 75, for a total of 295. Harry Vardon, James Braid and George Duncan were next in order of merit, and the leading amateur was the Hon. Michael Scott, who cannot have imagined that twenty-one years later, an unfamiliar Edwardian survivor, he would

win the Amateur Championship at Hoylake and, at 55, be the oldest
player to do so.

Taylor, Braid, Vardon and Herd had dominated the championship
since 1894. They were very much of an age, with Herd (born 1868)
slightly older than Vardon and Braid (1870) or Taylor (1871). The success
of Ted Ray, like Vardon a Channel Islander, marked the breakthrough
by the younger generation of professional golfers. The most impressive
feature of Ray's play was his spectacular length, and he demolished many
of the holes with his driver, his huge, saucer-faced niblick, and his putter.
His was a tremendously popular win, and he completed his final round of
75 amidst growing enthusiasm. Several spectators insisted on hoisting the
colossal form of the new champion on their shoulders and carrying him
off the green in triumph, a task that nearly proved beyond their capacity.

Let the 'triumvirate' and Alex Herd provide their own epilogue to this
chapter. J. H. Taylor's son, Leslie J. Taylor, who was for twenty-five years
assistant to his father at the Royal Mid-Surrey Club, is the witness to
another strange competition in which the four engaged. In 1962 he
wrote to Mr. D. J. R. Mackay, the son of the oculist who had tested the
eyesight of all four during an interval in the play at Muirfield:

> The facts, as I well recall my father telling them, are as follows. The four
> were, after a day's golf, walking along an Edinburgh street when
> Alex Herd complained that he had putted badly and said that he had
> not sighted the ball clearly on the greens and wondered whether it was
> due to his liver being out of order or to his eyesight becoming in any
> way impaired. This aroused the interest of the others, especially my
> father, who suggested that they all went together and have their eyes
> tested by a really competent man – with this strong echo of 56 years
> later.
>
> Furthermore, in a very non-technical style, I well recall what my
> father used to say was the result of their visit. Briefly, the one who had
> anything approaching perfect sight was Harry Vardon, with Alex
> Herd a good second. My father's right eye was very weak (he used to
> address the ball with his head turned slightly to the right) and James
> Braid's sight being the weakest of all. As regards the latter, it was a
> sort of standing joke between the other three never to concede a short
> putt to Braid as they considered it to be his golfing 'Achilles heel'.
> Also, at past 60 years of age, when he was still playing very fine golf
> indeed, he confided to my father that he then never saw the ball in
> flight after he had hit it, which is surely a fine testimony to your
> father's sight testing skill so many years beforehand.

CHAPTER VII

MAINLY TWENTIES AND THIRTIES

The immediate post-war period, culminating perhaps in 1926 when the first Amateur Championship was held on the remodelled course, seems in retrospect to have been a halcyon time at Muirfield. This was partly because the trumpet had been hung in the hall and efforts could now be directed to more peaceful purposes. It was in some measure due to the activities of the far-seeing men who served on the war-time Committee. They had fought a stern rearguard action against the inevitable decline in standards and facilities and had been planning ahead so far as circumstances allowed. It is also true that a club with a long history can, on occasion, inherit some indefinable but cumulative wisdom which it can put to use to guide its actions. This 'wisdom', mystique or attitude can sometimes be identified as an aura hanging over the head of the Captain at the Annual General Meeting: more progressive members have been known to wish the cloud would descend to engulf him. But as at all Gaelic discussions, there is something that is there but cannot be seen. In this case, it was the Honourable Company's diffident sense of maturity. But the real reason for the upsurge of activity in the early 1920s was that it was suddenly permissible, and tremendously agreeable, to play golf again.

The serene developments at Muirfield are also in contrast with the hectic atmosphere which soon began to dominate the scene during the twenties. This was the age of mounting economic difficulties, of the frenzied pursuit of speed (Malcolm Campbell and Henry Segrave were the heroes) and of growing national hysteria. Outwardly, there were detectable changes in dress, on the links as elsewhere. It was the age of plusfours, although they were scarcely considered to be respectable descendants of the elegant golfing knickerbockers of the past until they were worn by the Prince of Wales. His Royal Highness became an Honorary Life Member of the Honourable Company in 1926.

In April 1919, the valiant Mr. Charles Paterson, who had served the Honourable Company well throughout the war, passed over the captaincy to Mr. A. G. G. Asher. Two Committee members, Messrs. C. T. Dalziel and J. C. Couper, had also served during the whole period from 1914-19, and had been joined, during the war period, by Messrs. R. K. Blair, D. Lyell, D. A. Stevenson and J. J. Davidson. As an outward sign of the return to normality, Medal competitions and ballots for new members were resumed; vacancies were filled at a special Spring ballot. The Honourable Company was now once more up to strength, but the full majesty of the Club dinners remained in abeyance for some time. Only when new entries were made in the Bett Book would the members' proper habit of life be resumed.

The Minutes of the period are concerned with domestic trivia and the benevolent energy of the members. There is the well-supported story of one of them (Mr. R. K. Blair) who, being not wholly satisfied with the dryness of the sheets in the bedrooms, solemnly presented the Club with six hot water bottles. A good example of offensive, but constructive, criticism. Other Minutes pose questions. Why, for instance, was it suddenly necessary to order six dozen bottles of port? Was this to replenish the cellar after a visit by the Merchistonians, the first golfing society to return to Muirfield after the war? Or, more likely, was it to make good an understandable war-time decline in stocks? At this time, too, Lord Derby presented the Club with the 'Lanark Bell' which he had won with his horse 'Redhead'. His gift, symbolic of the genial atmosphere of the twenties, also recalled the former use of Muirfield's Hundred Acre Field as a racecourse, and the Bell is still kept in the small dining-room in the Clubhouse.

Out-of-doors, more golf was played than ever before. In order to emphasise that, though wars might come and go, a sound technique would last for ever, Robert Maxwell, who had won the last pre-war Medal in 1914, also won the first post-war competition held in October 1919. His round of 82 was two shots ahead of his old rival, J. E. Laidlay. Maxwell remained an impressive figure. He was made a Trustee in 1928 at the same time as another great personality from the past, his former rival John Ball of Hoylake, was made an Honorary Life Member. A few years later, Maxwell presented the Club with his golf medals, which had reached the remarkable total of eighty-four, together with a replica of the St. George's Challenge Cup which he had won at Sandwich as long ago as 1900.

The green staff had their numbers restored, and intensive warfare on the moles was resumed. Rabbits, however, were still a menace, and a trapping contract was let for £91 for the months from September to March. Three horses were still kept for pulling the heavy mowers, but a motor mower was also acquired at the exorbitant price of £400. The wages of Mr. Torley, the admirable head greenkeeper, were raised to 50s. a week; but it was not until 1926 that the Committee felt strong enough to authorise a member of the green staff to sweep the greens on Sundays for a special weekly bonus of 10s.

The Royal and Ancient, anxious to see the resumption of the major championships, had earlier enquired whether the Amateur could be played at Muirfield in 1919: but the Honourable Company, aware that there were still post-war obstacles to be overcome, and remembering earlier criticism of the length of the course, prudently pressed for a year's deferment. Before the war the Committee had been exercised over the growing difficulties of entrusting the increasingly complicated management of the Open and Amateur Championships to the host club. There really was too much to be done, and it became more and more apparent that a permanent organisation would have to be created. This was a matter in which the Honourable Company were concerned every few years when a national championship was held at Muirfield, and they seem to have taken the initiative in deciding that a new concordat was needed. After some informal discussion behind the scenes, helped by some of the members belonging to both clubs, the Honourable Company wrote in an exemplary manner to the Royal and Ancient in July 1919 –

> The Honourable Company of Edinburgh Golfers consider it in the best interest of golf that the time has now arrived that there should be a supreme Ruling Authority for the management and control of the game and to further this end they give notice that they will propose the following resolution at the next conference of Delegates from Open Championship Courses:—
> 'That the Royal and Ancient be asked to accept the management of the Open Championship.'

Two months later, the management of the Amateur Championship was added to the Resolution, and the problem was solved.

The windmill, which for long had seemed to hover like a protective bird over the links, was destroyed in a Spring storm in 1920, and some of the more superstitious members detected an ill omen. But, despite this, the course was in good shape for the 1920 Amateur Championship, which attracted 165 entries and was won by Mr. Cyril Tolley who beat Mr. R. A. Gardner from the United States in the final.

The only chill wind which had blown over Muirfield just after the war was the unhelpful reaction of the owner of the Dirleton Estate to a tentative approach by the Company to buy the links. This met with an emphatically negative reply and, since the lease was due to run out in 1926, there was some anxiety about the future. In 1922, however, the Captain announced, with some glee, that, after negotiations conducted in a most amicable manner, Colonel Ogilvy Grant, who had recently succeeded to the Estate, had agreed to sell the present links, together with a further 50 acres, to the Company for £8,500. Fortunately for their successors, the Committee decided to make the best of this unexpected opportunity and to lay out what was, in essence, a new course. Plans were commissioned from the golf architect, Mr. Harry Colt, with the advice of Mr. Robert Maxwell. All traces of the offending northern wall could at last be eliminated and a much more spacious field of play provided.

The work of reconstruction was carried on with determination throughout the following two years under the direction of a special committee consisting of three well-known Muirfield figures, Messrs. A. W. Robertson Durham, R. K. Blair and, inevitably, Robert Maxwell. The cost of the alterations, including drainage (no doubt in memory of Andrew Kirkaldy), fencing and the laying of a water supply to the new greens, came to £3,600. To complete these arid financial details, the Trustees were authorised to borrow £12,000 on the security of the links and Clubhouse and to raise the annual subscription to the unthought of figure of five guineas. The Honourable Company were now in a position to house both the Scottish Amateur Golf Championship in 1925 and the British Amateur in the following year. The outcome of the Scottish Amateur was particularly satisfactory since the winner, Tom Dobson, was one of the green staff and, with his new title, he soon left on preferment as professional at the East Renfrewshire Club. Lord Derby, always a good friend of Muirfield, wrote at the end of the year:

> I cannot resist congratulating you on the tremendous success of the new holes. They have made all the difference to the course and one no longer has the feeling one is playing round and round a field. It is perfectly charming.

The competition for the 1926 Amateur was, under the new dispensation, conducted by the Royal and Ancient, and the Honourable Company's responsibility was confined to general administrative and domestic arrangements. A large golf exhibition tent was pitched for the first time, and the charge of gate money (2s. 6d.) was made for spectators. The Honourable Company had argued against making a charge, but a somewhat quizzical Minute of the Royal and Ancient Championship Committee (23rd May, 1926) reveals that gate money was charged for the peculiar purpose of limiting the number of spectators and 'especially those ignorant of the game and therefore possibly difficult to control'. To modern eyes, this seems a slightly inhospitable attitude compared with the elaborate efforts now made to cater for the comfort of thousands of spectators.

Visitors to Muirfield – possibly irritated by a fruitless search for the non-existent professional's shop – often enquire why the Honourable Company does not, like most civilised clubs, have the services of a resident professional. They ask whether this is yet another annoying variant of the Club's indifferent anonymity. This is not, however, so. The main reason is a straightforward economic one. Most of the members of the Honourable Company are also members of other golf clubs, probably nearer their homes, and, if they admit that their swings are capable of improvement, it is there that they are most likely to engage a professional for beneficial instruction. The regular traffic on the course, except at weekends and during parts of the summer holiday season, would not be sufficient to engage the energies of a full-time professional. And the Honourable Company have always considered that, in these somewhat unusual circumstances, to engage a professional for the Club would be less than fair to the person appointed and would have an unnecessarily adverse effect on the professional at the nearby Gullane club, with whom cordial relations have always existed.

But Jack White, who had been professional at Sunningdale and Open Champion as long ago as 1904, nearly became the Honourable Company's professional. In 1928, since he was on good terms with many of the members, he asked for permission to open a shop at Muirfield. For the reasons already given, this request put the Committee in a dilemma. After much thought, they decided to accede to White's request, but with a number of stipulations attached. As it happened, one of the perquisites of the Clubhouse steward had always been the sale of golf balls to members and, since the Committee could see no good reason for depriving him of this revenue, one of the conditions prevented White from selling golf balls in his shop. This proviso was, however, found to be contrary to the Rules of the Professional Golfers Association: and the matter was dropped. The possibility of appointing a professional does not appear to have been raised again, despite fleeting complaints by those who are unable to remedy temporary deficiences in equipment. But at subsequent championships, Jack White, and later Hugh Watt of Gullane, have, in agreement with the Honourable Company, set up temporary shops on the course.

With the layout for the 1926 championship the Muirfield Green proved to have taken its permanent form, and alterations since then have been minor ones. From then until the outbreak of the Second World War, successive championships were played every few years without anyone making a fool of the course. Each one had its own particular flavour. Jesse Sweetser's Amateur Championship in 1926 had shown that, although the new holes were scarcely set, the course could survive a stern test. This was followed by another Amateur won by John de Forest in 1932. On a more modest plane, W. W. Mackenzie and, E. D. Hamilton won the Scottish Amateur Championships at Muirfield in 1928 and 1938 respectively. Walter Hagen's victory in the Open Championship in 1929 was a highlight, and the other Open before the war was, surprisingly, won by Alfred Perry in 1935. These championships are described in their context in the Bay Leaves chapters. Here, for our present purpose, it is perhaps sufficient to remark that the 1929 Open – perhaps awaiting the advent of Hagen and his fellow Americans – seems to have been the first which was organised on a straightforward commercial scale. The extensive catering arrangements outside the Clubhouse were undertaken by Fieffers, a leading Edinburgh firm of caterers. More and larger marquees were pitched round the Clubhouse; a new garage and car park on the east of the access road were made available; and, for the first time, the Automobile Association were engaged to supervise the car parking.

Early in 1933, Sir John Couper (who had been appointed a KCVO in 1930) announced his resignation as Honorary Secretary and Treasurer. He had held office for twenty-one years, including the whole of the exacting war period, and the Honourable Company decided to recognise his memorable service by appointing him to be the next Captain. Sir John has other claims to fame since, during his captaincy, for the first and only time the health of a lady other than the ruling Sovereign was drunk at a Club dinner. At the Autumn Medal dinner after he had assumed the captaincy, Mr. Robert Maxwell the senior ex-Captain present proposed the health of the Captain's daughter, Miss Millicent Couper, in recognition

SUMMER EVENING AT MUIRFIELD

of her winning the Scottish Ladies' Championship. The toast was drunk with enthusiasm and the Recorder was instructed to enter an account of this unprecedented event in the tablets of the Bett Book.

In Sir John's time it was also realised that the Club needed the full-time services of a Secretary, and Major G. W. Holt was appointed. An interesting period event was the decision, by 42 votes to 25, to allow caddies to carry clubs on Sundays: an unusual form of schizophrenia on the part of the members had allowed them to play golf on Sundays since 1903 but had rigorously proscribed the employment of caddies on the Lord's Day. This Calvinistic anomaly was now corrected.

The most notable change made in the course during all this time was the digging of Simpson's Folly. As part of the preparations for the 1935 Open, a well-known golf architect, Mr. T. Simpson, was asked to recommend whether any further unchristian hazards were needed for the better frustration of the competitors. He did his job well. On his advice, a single new bunker on the ninth fairway, forty yards from the green and some twenty yards from the wall to the south, was dug. Its siting is acknowledged to have been truly Machiavellian. Although it is one of the few hidden bunkers on the course, its enticing slender shape exercises a hypnotic effect on those who are aware of its existence and, frequently, in order to avoid it, the inexpert shot will go too far to the left and accordingly over the wall and into oblivion. Siren-like, it also attracts the low-running shot towards the green which will come to rest in its face. Those who avoid Simpson's admire his skill; but by his victims he is execrated.

In 1937, the Honourable Company received a letter from the Keeper of the Privy Purse intimating that H.M. The King had been graciously pleased to grant his patronage to the Club. As Duke of York, King George VI had been made an Honorary Life Member in 1929.

It has always been the prerogative of Captains to make minor alterations during their period of office which they think will improve the course; although it has to be admitted that such improvements as have resulted have often proved to be temporary and removed, with general consent, by their successors. It is against this background that, in 1937, the retiring Captain, Mr. Hall Blyth announced with pride that, during his tour of duty, no alterations had been made to the course. A post-war Captain (Mr. G. T. Chiene) could not make such a sanguine claim since, during his captaincy, but unknown to him at the time, the Secretary

G

planted two large clumps of daffodils beside the tenth and fourteenth tees. The Captain greatly deprecated these exotic flowers which he thought out of place on a golf course, but he did not feel strong enough to have them removed. Even at the time of writing, George Chiene's opponents find that it is worth two holes a round to admire the host of golden daffodils and draw his attention to their delicate appearance.

The Honourable Company seldom engages in team competitions, apart from an annual, and usually vain, attempt to win the East Lothian County Cup. Matches are admittedly played each year against the Prestwick and Royal and Ancient Clubs, but these are by sides chosen by the Captain for reasons which are not always confined to golfing prowess. In 1937, however, the Club played an intriguing match against a team of South African amateurs who were touring Great Britain. The match was notable for two reasons. First, an early appearance by their leading player, A. D. Locke, then described as 'the brilliant young South African golfer'; secondly, the superhuman golf by Captain (now Brigadier) W. L. Steele, who demolished Locke in the leading single by doing four consecutive holes in eleven strokes to finish the match with a win by three and two. The sequence from the thirteenth hole was 2, 3, 3 and 3. The length of the holes was 153, 458, 393 and 198 yards. In all his long and distinguished career, Locke can never have faced anything more frightening. The result of the match proved to be an amicable draw, and this event is thought sufficiently historic to merit the recording of the details:

FOURSOMES

Hon. Coy.		South Africa	
Major W. H. Callander and		A. D. Locke and	
Captain W. L. Steele	0	Otway Hayes (7/6)	1
Dr. J. Henderson and		C. E. Olander and	
J. D. H. McIntosh	0	F. O. L. Agg (2/1)	1
	0		2

SINGLES

Steele (3/2)	1	Locke	0
Callander (2/1)	1	Olander	0
Henderson	0	Hayes (8/7)	1
McIntosh (3/1)	1	Agg	0
	3		1
AGGREGATE	3		3

Meanwhile, all was at peace on the links under the expert supervision of Mr. Torley, who stayed in the Club's service for over thirty years until 1942. The last horse had disappeared, and the only concern seems to have been aroused by two constant menaces: the sandblow from Gullane beach on to the second green, and the obstinate prevalence of rabbits. Substantial buckthorn hedges were planted to the west of the second green and these have since been fortified by some first-class anti-erosion works carried out by the County Council. But when the wind blows hard from the west, the sand still stings the faces of those in the area of the green. Rabbits multiplied, as they do, and the Archerfield Estate complained that much damage was being done by burrowing under the walls at the eighth and ninth holes. The Secretary sent an ingenuous reply that, while the Club were doing all they could to reduce the rabbit population (1,310 couple were destroyed in a month in 1934), 'it was possible that an equally large number of rabbits were coming from Archerfield to Muirfield'.

Two more Captains were elected before the shadow of war descended again – the Hon. R. B. Watson in 1937, and Mr. (later Sir) R. H. Maconochie in 1939. In 1939, too, the Honourable Company won the County Cup for the first time since 1930 with a team consisting of Messrs. R. M. Carnegie, J. D. H. McIntosh, W. I. E. Thorburn and C. J. Y. Dallmeyer. The last Medal to be played before the outbreak of war was won by Mr. I. A. D. Lawrie with 77, Mr. G. T. Chiene winning the Silver Medal with 78.

Once more it was time for most golfers to put the shutters up, and the Club was kept in barely suspended animation until the end of the war. A moment of reflection, however, reveals that the Honourable Company, and the very game itself, were in a better state of health in 1939 than they had been a quarter of a century before at the outbreak of the First World War. The Open Championships at Muirfield had emphasised the great strides made by professional golfers, who owed a particular debt to Walter Hagen and Henry Cotton. Hagen, in particular, with his buccaneering flamboyance and his philosophical motto 'Never hurry; never worry; and always take time to smell the flowers on the way' had added an extra dimension to the popular concept of the golfing professional. Henry Cotton had imparted a new polish in more Anglo-Saxon terms. But if the professionals had done well, this was also the time which marked the fine flowering of amateur golf. Bobby Jones, although he never won at Muirfield, had shown that amateur players could still challenge the professionals, and there was almost as much public interest in the competition for the Amateur Championship as there was for the Open. Since then, the graphs have crossed; professional golf captures an ever-increasing share of public attention, but the public at large are much less interested in the outcome of amateur competitions.

At Muirfield the links had assumed what has so far proved to be their permanent shape. The texture of the fairways improved with the years and, since the disappearance of the wall, the slight feeling of claustrophobia, which earlier visitors had experienced, was no longer an embarrassment. Though Muirfield had produced no more Amateur Champions after Robert Maxwell, golf was still played very much in the spirit of the original Thirteen Rules, possibly with some slight maturing in the cask.

War-time activities can be briefly mentioned as a postcript. Dinners and Medals were suspended, and the green staff reduced. The grazing of the links for 250 sheep at a rent of £75 was agreed. During 1940, poles were erected on the grass to prevent enemy landings, and the Club were informed that trenches were to be dug as tank traps. But early the following year the Agricultural Executive Committee relented and informed the Club that arrangements need not be made for ploughing up part of the course. In 1942 Mr. Maconochie was replaced as Captain by Mr. R. Y. Weir, who said that 'It will be my endeavour to maintain Muirfield in good condition so that it might be available for the enjoyment of members serving in H.M. Forces when they return.' On 7th March, 1944, congratulatory telegrams were received from the Royal and Ancient and Prestwick Golf Clubs on the occasion of the Honourable Company's bicentenary. But this was no time for celebrations in the midst of war, and the only reference to the Club's commemorating their 200 years of existence was a decision that a graceful and concise summary of the history of the Club, which had been prepared by Mr. R. M. McLaren, the Recorder, should be printed and sent to all members.

CHAPTER VIII

BACK IN THE GROOVE

The first post-war Captain was Mr. J. A. Robertson Durham, who took over from Mr. R. Y. Weir in 1945. Mr. Robertson Durham, a distinguished golfer who had represented both Oxford University and Scotland, was the second, but not the last, of that name to hold office with the Honourable Company. Eighty-four members of the Honourable Company reappeared for the first post-war competition in May 1946 when the Gold and Silver Medals were won by Mr. P. M. Smythe (80) and Mr. C. D. Lawrie (81). The Spring Meeting in the following year was notable for the savage inclemency of the weather; a strong north-east gale blew with heavy rain and sleet all day, and competitors had to remove ice from their eyebrows without wincing. Seventy-one struck off from the first tee, but only sixteen shaken survivors holed out on the eighteenth green. The perils of this Wagnerian struggle were reflected in high scores appropriate to the conditions. Mr. Lawrie won the Golf Medal in 88 and Mr. G. Robertson Durham the Silver in 90 (after a tie with Mr. J. G. Dawson).

Mr. Stair A. Gillon, a former Captain, who had produced a pungent history of the Club over the period 1890 to 1914 (wisely, for private circulation), was made an Honorary Life Member. The same honour had already been conferred on Mr. C. B. Clapcott, who had done a great deal of detailed research into the history of the Honourable Company and produced various unpublished papers describing the life of the Club in the years 1744 to 1891. In 1947, the Captain reported that a further £290 had been received from the War Department for the depredations of the military and that all claims for war damage, amounting to £1,500 in all, were now settled. On a less cheerful note, it soon became apparent that the predictions of one of C. B. Cochran's war-time revues that

We'll soon be having nuts and caviare

Après la guerre, après la guerre,

would not readily be fulfilled. Because of the continued rationing of whisky, the following melancholy rules were posted for the reluctant compliance of members:

(a) Each member was to be allowed only one whisky on a Saturday and one on a Sunday:
(b) Members of the Bench and Bar were to be allowed one bottle per month to be served only on Mondays:
(c) Up to a limit of one bottle was to be reserved for members staying in the Club at weekends – the exact amount depending on numbers:
(d) At no other time and to no one else would whisky be available.

This, together with the gloomy news from the Agricultural Executive Committee that golf courses must again graze sheep, or be partly ploughed up for cropping, or sell the grass cut on the course for hay, was a sharp reminder that austerity still prevailed. The Club were fortunate in being able to sell their grass as hay and avoided the other less attractive suggestions.

Another pregnant event during Robertson Durham's captaincy was the appointment of a new Secretary. Major G. W. Holt, the Club's first full-time Secretary, had resigned in 1938 when his place was taken by Captain L. M. Kerr of the West Yorkshire Regiment. After military service during the war, Captain (now Major) Kerr returned to Muirfield in 1945 and served for a further two years until he resigned on translation to the Royal St. George's Club at Sandwich. He was succeeded by a distinguished cavalry officer, Colonel Brian Evans-Lombe. Secretaries of golf clubs vary in character. There are diffident Secretaries; there are unobtrusive, but efficient, Secretaries; and there are Secretaries who can be described only as imperious. Brian Evans-Lombe belonged emphatically to the last category.

He was exactly the right man for his time and no one could have guided the fortunes of the Club so skilfully through the lean years after the war. On arrival, he took a firm grip of the reins of office and when he relinquished them some seventeen years later, it was to everyone's regret. During this time he applied himself unsparingly to his duties, but although he did this with at least enough energy, his devotion to the interests of the Honourable Company was so transparent that he caused no offence. He was a familiar figure racing across the course on his bicycle if he detected some misdemeanour, a trespasser or a picnicker. More than one player felt that, if he failed to smooth out the sand after a bunker shot, he would come immediately within the optic lens of Brian's telescope. Early one Sunday morning he saw an unfamiliar figure sitting alone in the Smoking Room. Intending to make the imagined visitor welcome, Brian enquired whose guest he was, to receive the peevish rejoinder that he was addressing a member of twenty years' standing. 'In that event,' replied Brian, 'you should come more often: then I would recognise you.'

For visitors, particularly from overseas, Brian staged his own Son et Lumiere, and he delighted in conducting tours round the Club's sacred possessions – the original Rules, the Raeburn portraits, and so on. This he accompanied with a condensed history of golf and the Honourable Company. He would pause when he came to 1745 in order to explain that the most unfortunate effect of the Jacobite Rising had been to interfere with foursome play since not all the members supported the cause of Prince Charles Edward. One overseas visitor used to write every Christmas saying that his heart still bled when he thought of the Honourable Company having their golf spoiled by the vicissitudes of the Stuart dynasty.

In Brian's time, the Honourable Company used to require ties to be worn in the Smoking Room or the Dining Room (other appropriate neckwear is now allowed), and anyone who failed to bring a tie was courteously provided with one by the Secretary. Mr. Doyne Bell, a distinguished Harley Street specialist, arrived in mid-week with an introduction, and the Secretary arranged a partner who accompanied him on his morning round but had to leave immediately after the game was finished. Brian suggested that Mr. Bell should have lunch in the Club-house and that he would arrange for a second player to appear for the afternoon. Mr. Bell found this agreeable, and was peacefully drinking his gin and tonic alone in the Smoking Room. When he asked one of the maids to replenish his glass, she gazed at him with horror: 'Have you not got a tie, sir?' she enquired. Mr. Bell looked down at his foulard silk scarf knotted through a gold ring and sheepishly confessed that he must have left his tie at Greywalls. 'In that event, I'll see what I can do for you.' Such was the Colonel's influence that she felt compelled to go to the office and return with three scrubby cravats to invite Mr. Bell to make his choice. This he did, and lunched alone wearing, as he used to say, one of the original Victorian neckties.

Brian's consistency of purpose was also evident when the playwright

Terence Rattigan was introduced at Muirfield as a member of the Sunningdale Golf Club. 'That's very interesting,' said Brian. 'Did you know that Sheridan was born here?' Rattigan looked perplexed since he was unaware of any connection between the author of *The Rivals* and East Lothian; but he need not have worried – Brian was referring to Sheridan the caddiemaster at Sunningdale.

Invited as a guest to a meeting of the Monks of St. Giles, an association of amateur versifiers who meet regularly in Edinburgh to regale each other with their rhymes, Brian Evans-Lombe produced his own apologia:

> Club Members to me, I think you'll agree,
> Are as to a shepherd, his sheep;
> I chase them off here and pen them in there,
> And I count them as I go to sleep.
>
> I have to listen as their eyes glisten
> And they tell me of marvellous putts.
> All I've seen them sink, is a great deal of drink;
> It's gradually driving me nuts.
>
> They tell me with force what to do with the course
> And how drinks are cheaper in pubs.
> I'd like to suggest, if I ever was pressed,
> What they could do with their clubs.
>
> And when at last the ultimate blast
> Of the dear old trumpet calls,
> They'll all expect me on the first fiery tee
> With a box of asbestos balls.

Evans-Lombe served until 1964 when his resignation was accepted by the Honourable Company with real regret. He was elected an Honorary Life Member and is always welcome at Muirfield when he emerges on occasion from his retirement in Sussex. He was succeeded by Colonel George Elsmie, a Gordon Highlander, who carried out his duties with efficiency and in an aroma of Turkish tobacco. He had a great deal to do with the success of the 1966 Open Championship and remained as Secretary until he retired in 1968 to take up an administrative appoint-ment with his old regiment. Ill-health impeded his admirably ferocious approach to the game, but he remained unfailingly courteous and zealous at his work and is much missed by the members. As his successor, the Honourable Company were fortunate in appointing the present Secretary,

Captain P. W. T. Hanmer, R.N., whose nautical approach is easily discernible in Club affairs.

To return to the post-war years; in 1948, as normality gradually returned, the Committee appear to have observed that few members of the Honourable Company still made small pyramids of sand on which to tee their balls and, since peg tees were now used, it was no longer necessary to require the green staff to fill the tee boxes with sand. As usual, the Committee cannot be accused of being too precipitate in this, since sand had not actually been used since the twenties. This was the year of Henry Cotton's great Open Championship (described in Chapter IX). His Majesty, The King, attended for six hours on 1st July and honoured the Club by lunching in the Clubhouse. Following his visit, Mr. R. M. McLaren, the Captain, received a letter from the Private Secretary at Buckingham Palace:

My dear McLaren,
The King desires me to thank you and Members of your Committee for the excellent day which you provided for His Majesty at Muirfield. The arrangements which you made were ideal in that the King was able to see a great deal of good golf and to meet a number of interesting people without, at any time, being unduly thronged.
The King also wishes me to express his sincere thanks for the very good luncheon at the Clubhouse. I can promise you that His Majesty, and those of us who were so lucky to come in attendance, thoroughly enjoyed every minute of the day.
Yours sincerely,
(SGD.) MICHAEL ADEANE

The reference to luncheon does not tell the whole story since afterwards The King partnered by Major T. C. Harvey, The Queen's Private Secretary, played a match against the Captain and Guy Robertson Durham who had played well during the preceding days in the Open Championship. The King and Major Harvey received half a stroke and appropriately won on the last green, The King having holed his pitch at the fifteenth.

The match against the Royal and Ancient Club, which had not been played since the war, was revived in 1948. It was decided that it should take place every two years and that it would be a match between sides chosen, not strictly for golfing prowess, by the Captains. On this occasion, it was played at Muirfield and won by the Honourable Company by

eight matches to six, the sides being led by Mr. J. A. Robertson Durham
for the Honourable Company and Lord Teviot for the Royal and Ancient.

In 1951 the Honourable Company were surprised to receive the original
ball which had been driven at the opening of the Muirfield Green some
sixty years before. Mr. G. S. Smart, at one time Headmaster of Corbridge
School in Northumberland, who had no connection with the Club but
had been present at the opening of the course at Muirfield, returned it with
a letter which said:

> It was the first ball tee-ed at Muirfield. It was made by the late Tom
> Morris, Sen., and he wrote his name on it for me. It was tee-ed by old
> Crawford, a well-known caddy at that time who came from North
> Berwick, and it was driven off by Sir Alexander Kinloch, Bt. Old
> Crawford retrieved it and gave it to me in payment of a small loan.

By 1952, most post-war restrictions, rationing and regulations had
disappeared and there was a sense of looking forward. Mr. C. J. Y.
Dallmeyer, the new Captain who had succeeded Mr. P. C. Smythe, a
great post-lunch player and author of a delightful book on angling,
decided to alter the tenth hole. This was to be done by pushing the green
further up the slope behind the existing hole. It brought the play more
fully into view for the second shot; but the members never took kindly
to this innovation and, before long, the green was back in its original
place. In later years there were other projects to improve the course at the
eleventh, at the fifteenth (where a particularly whiskery kind of grass was
planted to fortify the rough) and at the seventeenth, where some artificial
pimples, known irreverently as the graves of the dead captains, were
erected in the rough on the left of the fairway. All these excrescences,
however, have since been planed away and the links restored to their
pre-1952 state.

About this time the Honourable Company first gave some prudent
thought to the necessity of taking such reasonable action as was open to
them to prevent encroachment over their boundaries. Golf courses are
greedy of land and they require more room than any comparable sport
or pastime. Because of their very extent and because they are usually sited
in pleasant rural surroundings, they are liable to attract the predatory
attention of those who want to propose that other use might be made of
the ground. Muirfield shares this situation with other golf courses, but
it has one advantage which is of crucial importance. The reputation and
history of the links are such that Muirfield can be regarded as a national

asset. During the periodic championships, crowds amounting to thousands come to the area and, in turn, contribute to local prosperity. This has been much in the forefront of the minds of the Honourable Company when considering acquisitions round their boundaries.

In 1952, Mr. Dallmeyer, supported by the advice of his Committee and the expert wisdom of Mr. Mackenzie Ross, the golf architect, earned the gratitude of the Honourable Company, their heirs and successors, by completing the purchase from the Biel Estate of the land between the north-east corner of the course and the sea. Three areas of this land (beyond the buckthorn to the north of the third hole, north of the fifth green and north of the tip of Archerfield) have since been leased to the Forestry Commission on terms which still enable the Club to retain control. The Commission's plantations will in time both provide additional shelter and help to serve as a bastion against sand erosion from the beach.

When, in 1954, it was thought desirable to provide a house for the Secretary, the Honourable Company purchased 'Quillet', with the surrounding ground to the south-west of the first green. Apart from providing quarters for the Secretary, this proved to be a far-sighted purchase. When the County Council decided some years later to feu the ground immediately to the south of the first fairway for private building, the Company were able to reach agreement with them to exchange some 3.7 acres to the north of the Secretary's house for a strip of land between the projected new building area and the first fairway. This exchange ('excambion' in Scots law) served two purposes. It provided much needed additional space for car parking during championships, and it enabled golf to continue along the first fairway without bringing the course under the very eaves of the new houses which were soon to appear.

Most clubs have a love-hate relationship with championships and the arrival of phalanxes of visitors to tread down the carefully nurtured turf, but the Honourable Company have never had much doubt where their predilections should lie. The observations of three different Captains can be said to sum it up. Mr. A. L. McClure (Captain 1956–57) sternly warned that:

From pure self-interest and on financial grounds alone, we must keep in the front rank. We belong to a Club and own a course which is envied everywhere as being one of the last places to be able to maintain the standards and traditions of the past. It should be our pleasure and our duty to keep this going as long as we can.

These impeccable sentiments were echoed by his successor, Mr. R. M.
Carnegie (1958–59), who was for long an extremely influential figure at
Muirfield. He bore a strange resemblance to an earlier great Captain,
William St. Clair of Roslin, and his outstanding captaincy was rewarded
with the presentation of a silver salver. In his view, Muirfield was

on the championship rota and the majority would like it to remain that
way. But a more important fact is that the R. & A. and the PGA are
very keen to have Muirfield for their championships.

This surprising unanimity among the Captains was maintained by
Colonel T. R. Broughton (1965–67) who delivered himself in even more
eloquent terms, admonishing the members as follows:

The question now arises whether we still want to be considered for
future Opens. The Committee are firmly of the opinion that any
inconvenience caused to members and the hard work which it entails
is more than compensated by the financial gains and the prestige it
brings to the Club. If Muirfield ceased to be a Championship Course,
the number of visitors, especially from overseas, would drop; Gullane
would suffer financially as well; members would lose the opportunity
of seeing the world stars play on their own course at little cost and
under reasonable conditions for spectating; and the Green Staff would
lose a great deal of incentive in keeping the course in first class condition.
Accordingly I hope you will agree with the Committee's view that,
if the Royal and Ancient consider our facilities adequate, we would like
to be considered for future Opens and any other major Tournament
which they, the Scottish Golf Union or other similar official Governing
bodies sponsor.

It would, however, be wrong to suggest that week in and week out the
golfers at Muirfield are preoccupied with such grim subjects as security of
tenure, or possible encroachment, or even the imminent arrival of
championships. Fortunately there are times when these items lack
topicality and the members can concentrate their energies on enjoying
their golf. A few more incidents in the last two decades bring the story up
to date. In 1953 Lady Sybil Grant added to the Club's exiguous collection
of trophies by presenting a cup in memory of her husband, the late Sir
Charles Grant, who had often played at Muirfield when he was G.O.C.-
in-C., Scottish Command. The cup has been awarded annually ever since
for the best aggregate scratch score for the Spring and Autumn Medals.
The first winner in 1954 was Mr. I. D. M. Considine; and the record is

143 (69 + 74) by Major David Blair, the Walker Cup player, in 1961. This was during the captaincy of Mr. J. R. Watherston (1960–61) who was the only Captain to be at the same time Master of the Edinburgh Merchant Company. Another trophy, with which the Honourable Company failed to make contact, was the Derby Cup awarded for an international competition among teams from the Senior Golfers Society, representing the United States, Canada and Great Britain. The contest for the cup was held at Muirfield in 1957 and Great Britain were the winners. It then happened that the Americans (the previous holders), who had brought a particularly strong team, had been strongly convinced of their likely success and had not brought the cup with them.

The growing number of foreign visitors who came frequently to Muirfield, and were anxious to enjoy a closer association with the Club, led to the introduction in 1958 of a new class of member whose place of domicile had to be outside the United Kingdom. Up to fifty foreign members can now be elected at the Committee's discretion and, with certain exceptions, they enjoy all the privileges of ordinary members. An extraordinary visitor in the same year was the Prime Minister, Mr. Harold Macmillan, the first holder of the office to visit Muirfield since Mr. A. J. Balfour. No wind of change blew over the links on that particular day, and those who saw the confident way in which he played his last pitch over the bunkers on to the eighteenth green were fortified in their view that the Government had not lost its nerve.

A few years later, in 1962, a visiting combined team drawn from the Oxford and Cambridge University societies was severely handled by a side drawn from the Honourable Company, led by Mr. McClure. In the morning, Mr. A. R. McInroy, playing for the Honourable Company, did the thirteenth hole in one without touching grass, his ball going full pitch into the hole. In the afternoon, Mr. Guy Robertson Durham did the seventh hole in one – the fourth time he had done so. But the statistical absurdity about all this was that both these holes in one on the same day were recorded against the same player on the opposing side, Mr. D. E. F. Simons.

Longevity is often a mark of the Muirfield man, but in none more so than in the case of Mr. Tom Drybrough who won the New Year's Day competition when aged eighty, fifty years after he joined the Club. He had been made an Honorary Life Member, and lunched in the Club on his ninetieth birthday in 1964. He was a fine example of all that was good in a foursome player and there was no more courteous partner. Two years later, two other senior members, Mr. D. M. Wood, who had been a member since 1918, and Colonel Thorburn, who had played since 1909 and at the time of writing still plays a respectable round, were also made Life Members.

The Hon. W. D. Watson, who became Captain in 1964, had earlier been responsible for staging an unusual match between the Honourable Company and the Royal Company of Archers. Mr. F. Tod and Mr. Archibald Blair represented the Honourable Company, and the Archers' representatives were Mr. Watson himself (he was also an office-bearer in the Royal Company) and Mr. (now Sir) Alastair Blair. The Archers were equipped with bows and arrows and, instead of holing out, were required to pierce a woolly ball placed at the edge of the green. The rules also said that they were to incur penalty shots if their arrow landed on the green or in a bunker. The long bow proved more accurate than even the best steel-shafted club and the Archers' side, who claimed to have gone round the course in 66, were well ahead of the Honourable Company. This friendly foursome brought the wheel full circle since the days of the Wapenschawe and King James I's proscription of golf for interfering with archery practice. There were no untoward incidents caused by driving, or shooting, into players in front.

Otherwise, bows and arrows are firmly banished and play at Muirfield keeps up with the times. There could, for example, be no sharper contrast with mediaeval archery than the recent marshalling of all the equipment required for the production of that most entertaining of artifacts, the television golf match. For this purpose, large numbers of technicians with cameras mounted on mobile gantries, producers, commentators, and their acolytes spend a whole day on the course. The programme, which lasts perhaps an hour on the screen, takes over eight hours to film. It is difficult to know what to admire more; the ingenuity of the cameramen or the prolonged concentration of the two golfers who can continue to play well nigh perfect shots at long intervals throughout a tiring day. The first match to be recorded in this way at Muirfield was in 1967 when Dave Marr from the United States played Peter Townsend. In the following year Muirfield was glad to welcome back Jack Nicklaus and Gary Player. The final conception so far in the television field has been the filming of a series of the best golf holes in Britain. For this purpose Tony Jacklin and Arnold Palmer, in the course of circumnavigating the globe, appeared very briefly one morning to be televised playing the ninth. No one disputes that, on any count, it still sets one of the most severe examinations in the golfing world.

Any year at Muirfield may see a mixture of old customs – the dinner Matches which are played in the same way as they were over 200 years ago – mingled with modern innovations; the television towers, the tented village and all the baggage train of an Open Championship. Jack Nicklaus sums it all up in his engaging biography, *The Greatest Game of All.* He first came to Muirfield for the Walker Cup match in 1959 and readily admits that, from the beginning, he liked it very much. He was impressed by the intrinsic qualities which it shares with other seaside links, fairways that 'tumble every which way', low-cropped turf and hard unwatered greens. He also welcomed the absence of hidden fairway bunkers or blind carries off the tee. Muirfield, he found, was a frank and open course. But, on his first visit, he was most impressed by the bunkers:

> They were, incidentally, the most fastidiously built bunkers I had ever seen, the high front walls faced with bricks of turf fitted together so precisely you would have thought a master mason had been called in.

When he returned for the 1966 Open and found the formidable rough (described in the next chapter), he decided that, in order to win, he would have to accommodate himself to the new condition of the course and to be ready to sacrifice distance for accuracy. This sudden burst of maturity, he says, was

> due to Muirfield itself. The memory of the 1959 Walker Cup was still fresh in my mind, I had never stopped looking back to it, not only because that match had changed me from a good junior golfer into a good golfer, but also because that whole week at Muirfield – the preparation for the match as well as the match itself – had personified sport at its best, people at their best, the world at its best. Okay, so the course was set up different in 1966 than it had been in 1959. It was still Muirfield, and if anyone could handle it, I could. After all, I was an old Muirfield man.

But this is looking too far ahead.

CHAPTER IX

BAY LEAVES (II) (1920–1966)

The first Amateur Championship after World War I, which had been postponed for five years during the hostilities, was held at Muirfield in 1920 and produced a sparkling final to celebrate the return of more peaceful contests. The Honourable Company applied themselves with some vigour to getting the course back into championship condition after the comparative neglect which it had inevitably suffered during the war years. There was, however, one problem which had evidently not been foreseen, namely, an acute shortage of caddies, and *The Times* commented acidly that those present were 'rather arrogant in their demeanour and extortionate in their demands' – a comment which is recorded because since then it would never have been justified.

The entrants included, at one end of the scale, the veteran Robert Maxwell, and spies on the course before play started had commented that his iron play was as good as ever 'and a few days ago he played a wonderful round which included nine threes'. At the other end, an entirely new school of post-war golfers was represented by Tommy Armour, then at the start of a remarkable career which included playing in international matches as an amateur for Great Britain in 1921, and as a professional for the United States in 1925. Armour, who always made much of his Scottish ancestry, later won the American Open in 1927 and the British Open at Carnoustie in 1931.

After three days' play, all the ex-champions in the field had been beaten, and the American peril, in the person of Mr. R. A. Gardner, was growing; although, as a contemporary report put it, 'One should not use such words about a visiting golfer who makes friends wherever he goes'. Gardner was a born athlete. He had held the world pole-vaulting record and had won the American doubles racquets championship. On his way to the final, he survived a cold semi-final day when he was seen practising iron shots in his great-coat to protect himself from a sharp East Lothian wind. But then he came up against Mr. Cyril Tolley of Rye, still an

H.M. King George VI at Muirfield, 1948

H.M. King George VI in front of the Club house, 1948

undergraduate at Oxford, who had already crowded a great deal of experience into a short golfing life. Strong as a bull, he could hit the ball out of sight, and he did it all with a fluent swing and smoking a curly pipe. The crowd were attracted by his natural authority. Tolley achieved the unusual feat of winning the championship at the first attempt when he defeated Gardner with a 2 at the thirty-seventh hole.

The 1926 Amateur will, ironically, be remembered for the unexpected defeat of Bobby Jones. As has been explained elsewhere, the whole shape of the course had been changed in the six years since the championship was last there. Bernard Darwin, writing in *The Times*, was generous about the new lay-out, but could not refrain from some characteristic astringency:

> This made a perfect setting for showing off the new Muirfield to the greatest advantage and there is no doubt that, as a test of golf in which long and accurate play receives its full award, it meets all requirements. The great attraction of the links, as they now are, lies in the new country nearer the shore which gives one a welcome sight of the sea and the pleasant coast of Fife guarded by its twin and misty sentinels, the Lomonds. As regards the links themselves, it is too early to give a considered judgment. As an old friend of Muirfield, one regrets the disappearance of well remembered features – notably the pond hole. One or two of the new holes seem a little artificial, a few greens rather billowing, but in time Muirfield will again take its place among the greatest links of the world.

The competitors included the American Walker Cup team, with a good field of home players, including Sir Ernest Holderness, Mr. Roger Wethered and Mr. Cyril Tolley (all of whom proved to be sadly off form) and the holder, Mr. Robert Harris. On the second day, the crowd, fewer in number than had been expected, and possibly deterred by the new entrance fee of half a crown, were palpably disappointed to see Gardner beaten by H. M. Dickson (Glasgow) by three and two. Gardner had endeared himself to all who had made his acquaintance on his last appearance at Muirfield in 1920. Like later American amateurs – Campbell and Hyndman come immediately to mind – Gardner's pleasing demeanour had led to his early adoption as a favourite son. But there was still Mr. R. T. Jones.

Probably no one has ever fascinated golfing spectators so much as Bobby Jones with his full, leisurely, classic swing and complete pivot. This must have been how golf was meant to be played. Bernard Darwin

H

had to confess that 'The rhythm of his style defies the prose labourer, or at least it entirely defies my powers of description'. It was sad that Jones never won a championship at Muirfield; but in 1926 it looked for a long time as though he would. In the third round he went out in 35, to beat Dickson by four and three; and in the fifth round he massacred the unfortunate Robert Harris by the margin of eight and six, playing golf which no one could have withstood. But, as Wodehouse would have said, even then Fate was slipping the lead into the boxing glove, and Jones was eliminated in the following round by Andrew Jamieson, Jnr., a young player from the West of Scotland, until then unknown in championship golf. Bobby Jones may have suffered from waking during the previous night with a stiff neck (though he scarcely mentioned it). Jamieson, however, was not to be denied his crowning glory and was level fours when he won.

After Bobby Jones' disappearance, the remainder of the championship went out with more of a whimper than a bang, and an agreeable American, Mr. Jesse Sweetser, beat Mr. A. F. Simpson from Edinburgh by six and five in the final. There was no doubt that, on the week's play, Sweetser, who was only the second American to win the British Amateur and the first since Mr. W. J. Travis in 1904, was the best player. The accuracy of his iron shots was decisive. He had some close calls on his way to the final, beating his fellow-American, Mr. Francis Ouimet, by a single hole in the third round, and only just surviving against the Hon. W. G. Brownlow (Addington) at the twenty-first hole in the semi-final. Poor Simpson started the final day under the worst auspices. His friend's car, which was meant to bring him from Edinburgh, did not turn up and he had to hurry down in a taxi. He was held up by a drove of sheep at Piershill and only just reached the first tee in time. Perhaps it is not surprising that he was never really in the hunt.

Walter Hagen wove his contribution into the Muirfield tapestry in the 1929 Open. This year the championship took place in May, much earlier than usual, in order to accommodate the American Ryder Cup team who were smarting from an unusual defeat by the British side. Qualifying rounds were played at Muirfield and Gullane No. 1 in driving rain and a gale sufficient to eliminate the infirm of purpose. So much so that an aggregate of 162 was good enough to qualify.

In the first round of the championship proper, Percy Alliss broke the record for the recently reconstructed course with a splendid 69. But, before long, Walter Hagen completed an even better second round of 67 (made up of 4, 4, 3, 3, 4, 3, 3, 5, 4 = 33; and 4, 4, 4, 3, 3, 4, 3, 5, 4 = 34). At the end of the first thirty-six holes, the leaders were the American, Leo Diegel (140) with an esoteric putting style which made him look like a contorted pine; Hagen (142), spruce as ever; Abe Mitchell (144), whose style and attitude recalled the days of Vardon and Braid; and Percy Alliss (145), who, on this occasion as on many others, flattered to deceive.

The morning of the final day, when two rounds were due to be played, broke with squalls and a gale from the south-west which, as though vindictively, completely altered the playing conditions. Before he started, Hagen confidently observed that two 75s would be good enough to win. One by one the earlier challengers were beaten by the elements, but Hagen steered the ball high, or low, as the wind demanded, to record a 75, one of the best rounds he had ever played. Diegel, following later, seemed to have putted his chances away with 43 for the first nine holes; he came back in a courageous 38, but was already five shots behind. By lunchtime the main interest had begun to centre on who would be second, and what Hagen's winning margin would be. The Master made himself even more secure with a precise outward half of 35. The only shot that was less than immaculate was a pulled second at the ninth hole which left him close up against the wall. He played an ingenious backhand shot to get himself out of trouble, but still took a 6. The second nine holes cost him 40 shots, but he almost appeared to be easing up. His second 75 for the day meant that he had exactly reached his target and that his estimate was no rodomontade.

Two shots which he played in the high wind of his last round remain particularly in the memory of those who saw him. First, there is the famous occasion when, standing on the eighth tee with the wind behind him, he saw the great rash of bunkers lying ahead and veering to the right, and he remembered that, in the morning, he had been short of the green with his second shot. A moment's reflection, and then he drove well out to the right into the rough, which had been trampled down by the spectators; saved distance by eliminating the dog-leg; and reached the green with a mashie niblick to hole out for a birdie 3.

Secondly, he played a chip to the fourteenth to demonstrate that, despite his enormous frame, no one could equal his delicacy of touch. He noticed that his partner's ball had curled off to the right, short of the green, and been blown further away by the wind. He had the worse side of the green to come from with the borrow running away from him; but he set his ball up against the wind to lie dead.

Hagen was the last man to win the Open using hickory clubs. The results showed that the Americans had obtained ample revenge for their defeat in the Ryder Cup. There were eight players from the United States in the first ten, and the first five were:

1st	Walter Hagen (USA) Holder	75, 67, 75, 75 = 292
2nd	Johnny Farrell (USA)	72, 75, 76, 75 = 298
3rd	Leo Diegel (USA)	71, 69, 82, 77 = 299
4th	Abe Mitchell	72, 72, 78, 78 = 300
5th	Percy Alliss	69, 76, 76, 79 = 300

The 1932 Amateur, so far as it is capable of being identified, is remembered not for the rough (which was very rough that year) nor for the absence of any colourful overseas competitors, nor for the dissipation of any remaining home interest with the elimination in the semi-final of the last remaining Scot, Mr. E. A. McRuvie. It is remembered as the 'slow championship' because of the tortoise-like behaviour of the two finalists. John de Forest, a very good golfer in his day, playing in the final for the second year running, won the championship by beating E. W. Fiddian, and *The Times* pronounced a just obituary:

Unfortunately the greatest drama is spoiled if it is played at too slow a pace and so this match, which might have gone down in history among the great finishes, gave an impression of drabness and weariness.

The thirty-five holes in the final had taken the incredible time of six and a half hours to play – a sad decline from twenty-three years earlier when Robert Maxwell and Cecil Hutchinson had delighted themselves and spectators alike by covering the course twice in four hours during one of the most memorable finals ever played.

The qualifying rounds for the 1935 Open (again played on Gullane No. 1 as well as Muirfield) started in conditions appropriate to the opening of Shakespeare's *Macbeth*. The courses were shrouded in a real vintage East Coast haar, and early starters could see at most fifty yards ahead. Competitors had to line up their shots in accordance with the ghostly voices of their fore-caddies percolating through the mist. These were real Gothic conditions and the greens were so wet with rime that long putts were better played with an iron club than with a putter. The rough oozed so much moisture that even the best shoes advertised in the Exhibition Tent were not watertight.

Henry Cotton, the holder, started at shorter odds than anyone since the days of Harry Vardon, and emerged from the Stygian gloom to share the qualifying lead at 141 with R. Burton. At the end of the first thirty-six holes of the championship itself, the leaders were Charles Whitcombe (71 + 68 = 139), Alfred Padgham (70 + 72 = 142), Henry Cotton (68 + 74 = 142) and Alfred Perry (69 + 75 = 144). H. Picard (USA), the leader of a foreign entry much smaller than usual, was on 145, and Mr. Lawson Little (USA), the British Amateur champion, was on 146. At the end of the day Alfred Perry of Leatherhead won with two fine rounds of 67 and 72 for a total of 283, with Padgham runner-up at 287 and Charles Whitcombe third at 288. Mr. Lawson Little was the leading amateur and his final 69 established a new record for the course.

It is no discourtesy to Perry to say that no one would have given very much for his chances at the outset; but this was his week and he was not to be gain-said. He had a curious grip with his right hand underneath the shaft and his swing had little aesthetic appeal for the onlookers, but on the greens he proved that the player who really intends to hole out and hits the ball firmly for the hole will win. In comparison with his resolute putting, the other leaders looked as if their real ambition was to avoid taking three putts, and this defensive attitude paid no dividends. Perry finished his final round with two glorious holes, striking the heart of both greens with determined wooden shots, and he never looked like taking more than 4 to each hole. Perry did not do quite so well again, but he was fully entitled to his moment of triumph.

Thirteen years and another World War were to elapse before the Open returned to Muirfield. The Royal and Ancient had suggested that the 1946 Amateur should be played there, but the Honourable Company, as at the end of the First World War, asked for more time to restore the course to its pre-war condition. In 1948, however, Bernard Darwin was finally prepared to concede that:

> the course looked in admirable order with the greens not too slippery after recent rain and plenty of sufficiently fierce rough lurking on either hand. I thought that there were even more bunkers than there used to be – I had not seen the course for ten years – but perhaps this was a senile delusion.

Regrettably, age was indeed affecting his memory, for the number of bunkers had not been increased.

Henry Cotton again led the qualifiers with 138 in cold, grey weather when the only cheerful glimmer of colour on the landscape was the vivid scarlet of the Loretto boys' stockings. The qualifiers included one Lorettonian, Mr. Guy Robertson Durham, whose father and uncle had both been captains of the Honourable Company. Only three amateurs, however, qualified for the final thirty-six holes: Mr. Mario Gonzales of Brazil, and Mr. F. R. Stranahan and Captain E. C. Kingsley, both from the United States.

One of the leading American professionals, Claude Harmon, entered Hermes-like from the Winged Foot Club in the United States, was entertained with something a little out of the general run. Harmon, who was an early starter at Muirfield, found that his partner had scratched. A hurried search in the Clubhouse for a substitute produced only a venerable member of the Honourable Company, Major W. H. Callander, late of the Royal Scots Greys. Callander, 'delighted to give the fellow a game', marched at once to the first tee. A large crowd of attendant newspapermen and photographers admired his martial mien, the gleam of his shoes which were always polished with more than oriental splendour and the aggressive way in which he smote the ball down the first fairway. After two peaceful holes (Harmon 4, 4: Callander 5, 5), the pressmen observed the two players engaged in some demonstration on the third fairway. Hurrying near to detect the cause of dissension, or perhaps to hear the terms of the altercation, they found, not a wrestling match, but a lesson in progress. Callander was generously supplying the wisdom of years of golf at Muirfield: 'Gripped further down the shaft, a short swing controls the ball more easily in the east wind'. Harmon benefited from, or at least survived, this advice to qualify for the final day's play with rounds of 75 and 73.

For the championship proper, the greens were becoming perceptibly drier and faster, and Cotton recalls them as being really like ice. At the end of the first day, C. H. Ward, F. van Donck of Belgium, and S. L. King led with 69, while Cotton and von Nida of Australia were lying handy with 71.

On the second day the championship was honoured by the presence of The King – the first time that a reigning monarch had attended such an event. His Majesty could not have chosen a more stimulating golfing day.

He saw C. H. Ward do the thirteenth in one stroke, and he was also there to see Henry Cotton set up a new course record with a 66 whose only blemish was three putts at the third. This put him four strokes ahead of the field, and the next day, with rounds of 75 and 72, he increased his leading margin to five and an aggregate of 284. This was Cotton's third win in the Open and perhaps his greatest. Bernard Darwin observed that, if he now retired, he would depart trailing clouds of great glory. For six rounds (including the two qualifying ones) he had been at his best, and had faltered only slightly in the third round. At the last hole of all, he gave his supporters a moment of anxiety when he needed two attempts to extract himself from a greenside bunker but, in confident fashion, he made amends by holing his putt for a 5.

Beside Cotton's triumph all else paled, but Fred Daly, the genial Irishman, was runner-up with 289. Roberto de Vicenzo from the Argentine had entered for his first attempt and, although at that time he knew no English, he was at once popular with the spectators, who rejoiced at his winning the Open much later in 1967. On this occasion he gave a warning of things to come by doing the seventeenth hole in two shots, a drive and a No. 3 iron. The growing public interest in the championship, which was no doubt increased by the chance of witnessing another win by Henry Cotton, was seen in the number of spectators which was thought to have reached 16,000 on the last day.

The last Amateur Championship to date to be played at Muirfield took place in 1954 and, since a Commonwealth tournament was due to be played at St. Andrews in the same year to celebrate the Royal and Ancient's bicentenary, the three hundred names entered for the championship came from all over the globe. The complete Australian, Canadian, South African and New Zealand teams were there, together with a strong American contingent led by F. R. Stranahan and W. C. (Big Bill) Campbell. The last eight had a good representative Commonwealth appearance – Joe Carr (the holder); one home Scot, A. M. M. Bucher (Elie); two Englishmen, E. B. Millward (Ferndown) and W. A. Slark (Walton Heath); D. Bachli (Australia); P. Toogood (Tasmania); and two Americans, Major Henderson and W. C. Campbell.

Toogood was unlucky to lose to Carr at the twentieth hole when the Irish holder of the title made the most of a surprising decision by the Championship Committee that his ball was in casual water and could be lifted and dropped without penalty. In the semi-finals, Carr and Slark were beaten by Campbell and Bachli. The final was an exceptionally agreeable one, with some fine precise golf. In the morning round, Campbell went out in 34, to be two ahead; but, after a more adventurous second nine, he lunched only one up. His first shot after lunch was one which many of the spectators could recognise as something they had often done themselves: it was a majestic top. Campbell, no doubt slightly upset, followed this with a hooked drive at the second hole which vanished into limbo. From then on, Bachli hung on to his newly acquired lead and, eventually, won by two and one. Good golf, and a good champion who had been in this country for only a week beforehand.

1959 was an exceptionally busy year at Muirfield. The Honourable Company had been disappointed that, after much preparatory work, the 1957 Open had to be transferred to St. Andrews because of the Suez crisis and the consequent rationing of petrol. In compensation, however, both the Walker Cup contest and the Open Championship were held at Muirfield in 1959, with only a few weeks' interval between them.

Every two years the New World sets about the Old with relish in what, though it is hard to admit it, has sometimes been almost a nominal match for the Walker Cup. It is depressing to have to record that, with a few honourable exceptions including 1971, the gulf between the sides has often been wide. Although the Americans have usually proved much superior, the Walker Cup provides the occasion for statesmanlike utterances about the special relationship between the two countries, and an opportunity for the Americans to look politely for Scottish ancestors.

It was so in 1959. The USA won all four foursomes over thirty-six holes on the first day, and what had appeared to be a strong British team, including Joe Carr, Michael Bonallack, Arthur Perowne and R. Reid Jack, was clearly at risk. On the second day, the USA won the singles by five matches to three for an aggregate of 9 to 3. The British successes included a fine win by Reid Jack against Billy Joe Patton, and the home crowd derived much entertainment and satisfaction from Joe Carr's win against Charles Coe in the leading single – although it was said that Carr really won because a Loretto boy had stood on his putter and broken it; as a result Carr went back to putting with his No. 3 iron and with success. To counterbalance this, the American Harvie Ward overwhelmed that very fine British golfer Guy Wolstenholme, and it cannot be said that the British side really looked like making much of a fight of it.

The reasons for the British failure were analysed by the Secretary of the

Henry Cotton, Open Championship 1948

AMERICAN TEAM

Back Row: T. D. Aaron, J. W. Nicklaus, H. Ward Wettlaufer, W. Hyndman III
Front Row: E. Harvie Ward Jnr, Deane R. Beman, C. R. Coe (*Capt.*),
W. J. Patton, Dr F. M. Taylor Jnr

The Walker Cup Match
between teams representing The United States of America and Great Britain
was played 15-16 May 1959 at Muirfield, Gullane, Scotland

BRITISH TEAM
Back Row: D. N. Sewell, A. E. Shepperson, M. F. Bonallack, M. S. R. Lunt,
D. M. Marsh, W. D. Smith
Front Row: A. H. Perowne, J. B. Carr, Gerald Micklem (*Capt.*), R. R. Jack, G. B. Wolstenholme

Gary Player, Open Championship 1959

Honourable Company, Colonel Brian Evans-Lombe, and recorded in the Minute Book. He points out that the British team played the first two and last two holes so badly that uncanny success elsewhere would have been needed to give them a chance. In the foursomes, only one British couple won the first and second holes in either round, and one couple went a complete misère and lost them both in the morning and afternoon. In the eight singles, no British player gained an overall advantage at these four holes, and in six out of eight matches, the Britons lost up to three holes. Colonel Evans-Lombe deduced that the British were incredibly poor starters and horribly indifferent finishers. On the green, the Britons were nearly always short and seldom past the hole, while the Americans always seemed much more aggressive. Some of the Honourable Company were arrogant enough to observe that Britain would have done better if middle-aged members had done the putting. Playing in the last foursome and single for the United States side was a young amateur who seemed to mock the longest holes with the power of his mighty shots. His name was J. Nicklaus.

Another young golfer, Gary Player from South Africa, won the Open Championship seven weeks later. Although it was his third attempt at the Open, even then he was only twenty-three and was the youngest winner since the event came to be held over seventy-two holes in 1892. In the preliminary excitement of the qualifying rounds, Peter Thomson of Australia, the holder, equalled the Muirfield record of 66, while Mr. Joe Carr blarneyed his way round Gullane No. 1 in 64, lowering the professional record by three strokes and the amateur by four.

Player's performance on the final day was superhuman. With thirty-six holes to come, Player was eight strokes behind the leader, F. Bullock of Prestwick St. Ninians, and had gained only one stroke on him after nine holes: but he came back in 33 without a 5 on his card, and reduced the deficit to four. There was still much to play for but, in the afternoon, Player began to scent victory. He went out in 34 and, on the way back, needed two 4's for a 66. His second to the seventeenth soared over the caverns, and his 4 was secure. But, for the only time during the day, he showed some human failing at the last hole, driving into a bunker and taking three putts for a 6. This gave him a round of 68 and an aggregate of 284 which, at the time when he finished, was by no means safe. There followed an agonising wait until the challengers had all failed to catch him. Flory van Donck (Belgium), a beautiful golfer who could never quite win the Open, was joint runner-up with Bullock at 286, and S. S. Scott (Roehampton) was fourth with 287.

This was, however, a championship where the few amateurs who qualified for the final thirty-six holes surpassed even their friends' expectations. With one round to go, Reid Jack (Dullatur) and Michael Bonallack (Thorpe Hall) were lying equal third. In the final reckoning, three amateurs finished within seven strokes of the winner, Jack being equal fifth at 288, Bonallack was on 290 and Guy Wolstenholme on 291. The two elder statesmen, Messrs. Gerald Micklem and Raymond Oppenheimer, who had derived little comfort from the results of their team's careful preparation for the Walker Cup, were entitled to some satisfaction for the brave showing by the British amateurs in the Open.

By 1966 it was all too evident that the Open Championship, due back at Muirfield again after an interval of seven years, was competing – still successfully – with other tournaments in a highly competitive big business field. In order to maintain the Open's prestige among other world championships, a positive effort was now needed to attract the best players on both sides of the Atlantic and from the Commonwealth. This meant more prize money and, in order to provide it, more spectators and the sale of television rights. So, for weeks before the championship started, an anvil chorus rang out over the links as the merry workmen hammered out tubular stands beside the fifth and ninth greens and on both sides of the last fairway. (There was even a small stand over the Clubhouse Smoking Room whose grotesque effect was redeemed only by the superlative vista from it towards the eighteenth tee.) A gigantic tented village sprang up to the north of the first hole; exhibition tents, bars, mobile banks, closed circuit television; the whole gamut was there and Muirfield looked more like Epsom Downs on Derby Day than a golf course. It needed a W. P. Frith to paint it.

Two new tees were constructed to make the course more exacting: at the sixth, where the tee was moved 150 yards towards Archerfield Wood which made bunkers on the left of the fairway more threatening; and at the seventh, where the tee was brought back 30 yards, or so, to make the hole more of a test against the prevailing west wind. The most controversial decision was made by Mr. Gerald Micklem, as Chairman of the Royal and Ancient Championship Committee, to allow the rough to grow in some places to waist height, and to narrow the fairways to as little as eighteen to twenty yards in places. This was the most ferocious rough ever seen at a British Open, described by Jack Nicklaus as looking 'like a wide expanse of wheat whipping in the wind'. There was not a little criticism from those who had lost their balls, their equipment or even their partners in the various strips of jungle. Rain before play started made the growth even more luxuriant. On reflection, the rough might, with advantage, have been graded from the edge of the fairway outwards, and on the last day three notable victims in quick succession (Lema, Palmer and Rodgers) were seen committing suicide by attempting to play long irons from the depths of the hay on the left of the tenth fairway. But, as Henry Cotton observed, if the rough was really too severe, how did it happen that there were many scores under 70, including a splendid 65 by Peter Butler? Cotton's conclusion was that the golfers were so appalled at the formidable appearance of the undergrowth that they began to think defensively. Nicklaus 'ironed' his way round the course, using his No. 1 wood only seventeen times in the four rounds; Arnold Palmer did not break 70 until he brought his driver more into play. On the other hand, Dave Thomas never hesitated to take a driver when it was needed. He was one of the very few to drive consistently over all the hazards from the new sixth tee and, on one occasion, at the eighteenth, he hit a drive which was measured as being all of 375 yards.

Each of the four days of the championship had its own excitement. At the start, an unfortunate Italian, playing in his first Open Championship, suffered the indignity of entering a 9 on his card at the first hole, including two desperate hacks from the rough. A later supplication to the gods enabled him to do the thirteenth in one, but this was not enough to let him qualify for the final thirty-six holes. The rough soon started to take its toll, but Nicklaus and Hitchcock recorded 70s, with fifty players behind them with 74 or less. The amateurs did well on the opening day: Ronnie Shade with 71 and R. Cole (South Africa), Michael Bonallack and Peter Townsend with 73.

The second day was dominated by Peter Butler with his round of 65 (finishing with a spectacular 3) to bring him into second place behind Nicklaus. Butler was drawn to play with Nicklaus on the following day and this and the large accompanying crowd may have put him off. He declined sadly to an 80.

The third day, with the field reduced to sixty-four, including four amateurs, belonged emphatically to Phil Rodgers. After going out in 40, he came back in an impossible 30, made up of 4, 3, 4, 2, 4, 3, 2, 4, 4, including six single putts. Rodgers was a sound, methodical golfer, but this was a day when the hole appeared to be the size of a bucket and he could not miss. At the end of the day, Rodgers was on 210, followed by Nicklaus (212), Sanders (213), Palmer and Dave Thomas, the only home challenger with a chance, on 214. The four best golfers on the week's play were now under starter's orders for the final gallop.

Rodgers' lead vanished at the first hole on the next morning. He had trouble with the rough and gradually faded away with a 76. Nicklaus and Thomas both started with birdie 3's, and it was clearly going to be a tense day. The present-day habit of matching the leading players together to come in at the very end of the last round greatly increases the entertainment value and imparts something of the quality of match play to the stroke competition. Most of the final quartet knew what the others were doing throughout their last round. With six holes to go, Nicklaus was two ahead of Sanders and Rodgers, and three ahead of Thomas and Palmer. Rodgers and Palmer were soon to fall; Rodgers with another 6, and Palmer with his own personal tragedy in the rough leading to a 7. But an enormous roar from the crowd signalled a birdie 2 for Thomas at the thirteenth to let him draw level with Nicklaus. At the sixteenth, Thomas's bold tee shot struck the pin, but he failed to sink his putt for a birdie. He finished with a heroic 69, his second at this figure, to be level with Sanders on 283 – the leading score.

Now came the real moment of truth. Nicklaus, playing as the last couple with Rodgers, who was now out of the running, had a birdie at the seventeenth and needed a 4 at the last hole to win. The excitement was such that some of the last players to finish, who were already in the Clubhouse, on learning what Nicklaus had to do, doubted whether this was within his, or anyone else's, power, and began to congratulate Thomas as joint-leader. This explained Thomas's understandable, but unconcealed, disappointment later. To come back to Nicklaus: thousands of spectators crowded into the stands on either side of the fairway. As Nicklaus made his lonely way back to the tee, the green in the far distance must have seemed a long and dangerous way ahead. He knew, too, that, while the crowd were fair and generous in their applause, there were very few who would be disappointed if Thomas won. A testing hole at the best of times, the eighteenth can seldom have been more difficult to play. Nicklaus elected to play a No. 1 iron from the tee as he had done all week. This left him with a No. 3 iron shot to the green. A few of his slightly irritating wiggles, and he was dead on target. The stands rose to him as he came confidently down the fairway with the admirable Rodgers, who was now fully resigned to his supporting role. Rodgers quickly holed out first to leave the way clear for the champion designate. Then it was Nicklaus's turn and there was never any question of his taking three putts; the first putt was adequate and the second was rapped firmly into the hole.

This had been a great championship, not only because it is still fresh in the memory, but because everything went well. The painful preparations which had been made beforehand produced such large gate receipts that the Committee increased the prize money by 20 per cent in the course of the championship to £15,000. Logan could be proud of his work as greenkeeper. Henry Cotton, writing in *Golf Illustrated*, observed that: 'I thought that on the final day our seaside golf heritage was offered to players and spectators alike at its supreme best'. But, much though they valued Cotton's praise, perhaps the tribute which the Honourable Company liked most came from someone who had often been critical in the past but who now wrote in *The Field*:

> The Honourable Company of Edinburgh Golfers, which for more than 200 years has been the name of the Club which now plays at Muirfield, have always kept themselves to themselves. After all, it is their Club and long may they be allowed to preserve their rules and customs. But they have courted criticism in the past at Championship time and sometimes it has been justified.
>
> This time, Micklem insists, the resounding success of this Championship was due entirely to the members of the Honourable Company who, by their own contributions, set out to make the Championship the best to date, and they did.

At the prize-giving ceremony later, Colonel T. R. Broughton, (the Captain of the Honourable Company), after paying the ritual, but richly deserved, compliments to those who had earned them during the week, extended a felicitous invitation to the new Open Champion. He invited him to come back and play in a foursome at Muirfield: 'You will be my partner, and I can assure you that you will play shots from country much more savage than anything you found this week'.

CHAPTER X

WAGERS AND GAMBOLS

Although few people have ever scrutinised its pages, the Bett Book has always intrigued those who know of its existence. There is some interest in examining any wagering ledger since a study of other people's follies ('How could he have hoped to win that one? It was clearly not a match.') confirms the superior judgment of the reader. Then, the continuity of the Honourable Company's Bett Book has in itself some merit; all the volumes, from 1776 to the present day, are still in the Company's possession. Lastly, the book casts some light, not only on the ambitions of individual members, but also on the changing temper of the times. Bets recorded in the book are all made at Club dinners, and the bill for a dinner at Leith in 1801 shows something of the comparatively expansive tastes of the members at the beginning of last century:

Dinner (14 dining)	£2.	0.	0
Bread and Biscuit		2.	0
Port, Ale and Spruce		8.	0
Gin and Brandy		6.	8
Port and Sherry (7 bottles)	1.	13.	6
Claret (16 bottles)	5.	12.	0
Tody, Glasses, Wax Lights and servants		11.	2
City Officers etc			
Dinner – Port, Rum and Tody		18.	8
Club and Ball Maker and Caddies		10.	0
Waiters		12.	0
	£12.	14.	0
To be paid by the Club		4. 6.	0
Remainder by 14 diners @ 12/–		8. 8.	0
	£12.	14.	0

The Bett Book originated from dinners held after the members' activities on the links on their 'Play Days', which were normally Saturdays. After the day's play, a dinner was held – initially in Clephan's Tavern and then in the Golf House at Leith – at which matches were made for the following weekend. The matches were recorded in the same book as that which kept the Club's general minutes, but an entry dated 4th January, 1766, is testimony to the growing practice of bets on matches:

> Each person who lays a bett in Company of the Golfers and shall fail to play it on the day appointed, shall forfeit to the Company a pint of wine for each guinea unless he gives a sufficient excuse to their satisfaction.

In 1776 the Bett Book was started as a separate volume and seven years later a 'Clerk to the Betts', who has been known as 'The Recorder' since 1785, was appointed. No one was to presume to write in the Bett Book when the Clerk was present. The first one was Mr. John Gray, the City Clerk of Edinburgh, who was described by Lord Cockburn in his *Memorials* as a 'Judicial man with a belly, white hair and decorous black clothes, famous for drinking punch, holding his tongue and doing jobs quietly'. John Gray was held in such affection by the Honourable Company that a portrait of him by Raeburn was commissioned and hung in the Clubhouse. Unfortunately, it was sold in 1831 and only a print of it remains in the Company's possession.

Since 1785 there have been only twenty-seven Recorders, which is itself evidence of their surprising devotion to their onerous task. Some, like James Mansfield (1882–88), are remembered for their grace and social qualities; others, like Ben Hall Blyth (1888–96), for their more stentorian approach; and others, like the present Recorder, for their simple wit. All have had to be alert to note the bets which the members dining wanted to make on a particular match; accurate in balancing the books; and phlegmatic in dealing with representations. Of these qualities, none is more necessary than a quick eye and ear in taking down the bets as they are proclaimed, and a stint as Recorder would qualify anyone for a job at Tattersalls.

Most bets have been made on foursome matches but, when the wagering fever has reached its height at the end of the dinner, it is not unknown for bets to be laid on events like the University Boat Race or the Calcutta Cup Match. The Honourable Company have never, however, gone so far as two of the bets which appeared in the Royal and Ancient Bet Book. There it is recorded that, in 1822, Mr. Bruce of Grangemuir successfully wagered that he would produce a leg of mutton at the September meeting better than one produced by Mr. Haig of Seggie, with a magnum of port to the Club as stake. Also in 1822 there is a record of what must be regarded as the ultimate bet when Sir David Moncrieffe backed his life against that of Mr. John Whyte Melville, the survivor to present a new silver club to the St. Andrews Golf Club.

An early entry in the Bett Book had fixed '100 merks on the day's play, or one guinea the round' as the maximum stake and, in 1778, there is the record of a match for '100 merks a corner and dinner for the Company'. The expression 'corner', as defining the personal obligation to each opponent in a foursome match, is accordingly of greater antiquity than is generally supposed. 100 merks would be equivalent to approximately £5, which is still a common stake.

A more eccentric bet is recorded in 1783:

> Mr. R. Allan betts one guinea that he will drive a ball from the Castle Hill without the gate of the palisade into the Half-Moon battery over the parapet wall

and did so. In the same year there was a wager that Mr. Robertson would

> compleat the round (5 holes at Leith) in 35 strokes for twelve guineas. Taken by Mr. Guthrie and lost by Mr. Robertson by one stroke.

Mr. Robertson was described elsewhere as an average player and he was setting himself a fair task since all the holes at Leith were over 400 yards long.

It appears that during 1793 some aggrieved member was beaten by someone too fainthearted to use his wooden clubs and managed to persuade the Honourable Company that timid play confined to irons should not be allowed:

> It is the unanimous opinion of the Company that no member shall play on the Links with irons all, without the consent of the Captain and Council and it is recommended by the meeting that they will not grant the desire of such application.

It is normally the rule that matches can only be arranged between those who are actually present at the dinner when the match is proposed, but there seems to have been an exception in 1797 when Mr. Alex Wood,

Jack Nicklaus, Open Championship 1966

The Spring Silver Medal

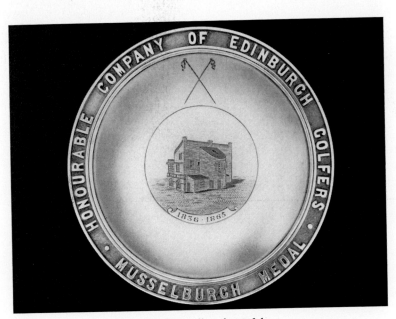

The Musselburgh Medal

then in his seventieth year, partnered by his grandson aged 7, defeated Dr. Duncan, a stripling of 50, and his son aged 5.

While singles were seldom favoured by members at dinners, in 1801 a match was recorded between Mr. Armstrong, playing with one hand, and Mr. Dunbar:

Won by Mr. Armstrong, Mr. Dunbar never gaining a hole and halfing only one during the match.

On 28th December, 1808, a match was proposed:

between a team of married Members led by the Captain (Mr. John Taylor) and a team of Bachelors, to be played on 8th January, 1809, for a claret dinner in the Club House that day – each individual in the party on either side is to play in a rotation to be previously fixed. If any individual one or more of either side absent themselves, his or their strokes are to be counted against the party as if they were present, but if the party loses the absentees pay double any of the rest of either party.

It is, however, recorded that Mr. M. Gordon, perhaps restrained by his spouse, failed to appear, and the bachelors, playing seven against six, won by six holes. Since a Club match at Leith was normally three rounds of five holes each, Mr. Gordon's defection must have been directly responsible for his side's defeat. He must have been doubly unpopular. This is the only recorded team match made at a dinner.

All the early Club matches were played at Leith, but one of them did not take place, and the defaulter was duly fined. The record for 16th July, 1803, states that:

Mr. Mitchell to play Mr. Rose next Saturday giving him one stroke each hole for a gallon of Highland Whisky. Mr. Rose appeared on the Green, Mr Mitchell did not.

It was resolved by the Captain and Company present that whoever was guilty of such an offence shall be fined in double of the bet and that as it was play or pay, Mr. Mitchell shall be answerable to Mr. Rose for the gallon of whisky which the Meeting recommended to Mr. Rose to produce at the Meeting of the Club next after he receive it.

The first match played at Musselburgh was in 1808 between the Captain (Mr. John Taylor) and Mr. Cook. It is not clear whether the indignant denunciation in the *Statistical Account 1845* referred to the Honourable Company or to other golfers at Musselburgh, but the chapter on the Parish of Inveresk complains that:

I

It is much to be deplored, however, that an exercise in itself sufficiently stimulating, should frequently be prostituted to the purposes of gambling, and that so many of the young who are employed as *cadies* or club-carriers, should be initiated in the practices of vice partly from the evil example of those in whose gambling transactions they take a deep interest, and whom they in this respect on a smaller scale ludicrously imitate, and partly from the mistaken liberality of their employers, who, by extravagantly overpaying them for their services, not only furnish them with the means of vicious indulgence, but totally unfit them for the sober and steady industry of any laborious calling.

The matches have, as a rule, been played on the Club's home links, but there have been expeditions recorded to courses as far afield as Islay, Formby, Hoylake, Sandwich, Walton Heath and Portrush. A game at Portrush in 1967 inspired the Recorder to provide a dithyramb which might rank as a spurious addition to Thomas Mathison's mock-heroic epic 'The Goff' (1743):

Unto the links of ROYAL PORTRUSH the flower of SCOTLAND came
To fight a mighty challenge at the world's most skilful game.
The top man there was MEIKLE, a fearsome player he
Who had as partner for the match smooth swinging JACK MACFIE.
Present too was BROUGHTON, a man of martial fame
Together with that Celtic ace, A. J. O. MAXTONE GRAHAM.
Here was a blend of strength and guile, of knowledge dearly bought,
Tempered by experience and matured in IRISH PORT.
It was a battle of the GREATS, a contest for the GODS
Though cynics said two rounds at all required a shade of odds.
Eye witnesses are hard to find, the leprechauns won't say
What happened on the noble links throughout that famous day.
With fearful oaths and flailing clubs the gentlemen progressed
As though with many demons they had all become possessed.
It was as well, the locals said, they all were in their prime
And also that the match was played in double summer time.
Though news on earth is somewhat vague, an official source in heaven
Assures us that MACFIE and MEIKLE won by eight and seven.

A more bizarre match was recorded as a single on 5th February, 1828, between the Secretary and M. Samuel Messieux, to take place at St. Andrews, each in striking to 'stand on one foot in the month of May'. Messieux also features in the records of the Royal and Ancient Club. He was a Swiss who came to Dundee in 1815, shared lodgings with the poet, Thomas Hood, and taught French at Madras College, St. Andrews. He is remembered for an enormous drive at St. Andrews which was measured as being over 360 yards: but, like some other big hitters, he was a poor putter, as the author of 'Golfiana' (1833) mentions:

Here's Monsieur Messieux, he's a noble player,
But somewhat nervous – that's a bad affair,
It sadly spoils his putting when he's pressed,
But let him win, and he will beat the best.

Play or pay has always been the rule and any member who might feel inclined to disengage himself from an unpromising commitment would be deterred by realising that his name would go down to posterity in the Bett Book, as happened on 9th February, 1880: 'C. v. M. Not played. C. funked.' The Captain keeps a careful watch on the matches proposed and none can be made without his permission. If the game seems unfair – and no strokes are given on either side – he will hammer it. Such occasions are few, but there is the record of one in 1886 when a game proposed between Mr. J. E. Laidlay and Mr. T. R. Menzies, the latter to be declared the winner if he succeeded in winning three holes in 27, was ordered to 'be not recorded'.

It is not, however, the stake-money which is the primary objective, and he who comes to dinners with financial appreciation as his main intention will soon be disillusioned. The matches have to be fair enough, and the outcome sufficiently uncertain, to attract wagers from those present. No strokes are given and this has long been the rule. The Bett Book for 1891 states that the Recorder 'had examined the record books back to 1865 and had not found a single case of a match recorded in which odds were given by one side to the other'. In order to ensure even matches, players of varying handicaps are partnered. In short, the system ensures that the most mediocre golfer can enjoy the excitement of the dinners and make matches with a good golfer as a partner and play his part, man for man, against, say, two average players. Most veteran diners confirm that at the end of the day, they have won or lost very little. One former Recorder, who recently played his 500th match, calculated that he had won a fraction over 50 per cent of them. A more recent Recorder found that his tally over 300 matches was within a decimal point of the same result. It is true that in 1958–59 Mr. M. M. Stuart played twenty-one matches without defeat; but that is the kind of statistical oddity that occurs from time to time.

The Rev. John Kerr's conclusion on the procedure followed at the dinners is still valid. He found that match play brought out all that was best in golfers. The parties engaged had not only themselves, but also their supporters, to vindicate, and not only their opponents, but also their opponents' friends, to overthrow. They therefore played for all they were worth, determined to win. This, and the fact that victory or defeat stood recorded for ever in the book, made the game very keen. Let Mr. Horace Hutchinson add a postscript:

> When playing a foursome, do not remind your partner about his bad shots until the game is over. You may rest assured that he did not foozle the ball on purpose; and even a gentle reminder is only apt to increase his anxiety and you never know when you may be guilty of a similar error yourself. An anxious player never makes a good foursome partner; he only irritates both himself and his partner and irritation is fatal to a successful combination.

Seven dinners are held each year. In the winter they are normally held, by courtesy of the Managers, in the New Club, Edinburgh; and through-out the rest of the year in the Clubhouse. Arrival on a summer evening, with a generous view of the links and the Firth of Forth lit with sunset colours, makes a good beginning. Then there is the ceremony of greeting the Captain who, like ex-Captains who are present, wears his red coat of office. As the diners assemble, matches are arranged for formal proposal later in the evening. During this elegant ritual – or oriental bazaar, depending on how you look at it – the portraits of former Captains hung on the wall of the Smoking Room look down like the ancestors in Ruddigore.

Clockwise round the room, the first is the Raeburn portrait of Alexander Keith of Ravelston and Dunottar (Captain 1768 and 1780) presented to the Club by A. J. O. Maxtone Graham, a relative of Keith's. This is one of Raeburn's truly enormous studies; the imperious figure of Keith is shown standing against an imaginary romantic background. Immensity is the main impression, and Keith does not appear the kind of person one would lightly challenge in a Club match.

Next comes another Raeburn of William Inglis (Captain 1782–84). This portrait was purchased by the Club in the 1950s from subscriptions raised by the members for the purpose. While the money was being found, it was alleged that this was perhaps not a genuine Raeburn, and Mr. D. K. Baxandall, the Keeper of the National Galleries of Scotland, kindly

THE PROCESSION OF THE SILVER CLUB

The Silver Club, presented by the City of Edinburgh to The Honourable Company of Edinburgh Golfers in 1744, was played for annually. The Victor became Captain of the Golf and arbiter of disputes touching the Golf. Each Captain, on completing his term of office, adds to the Silver Club a silver ball with his name on it. As each club has become loaded with balls the City of Edinburgh has presented a new club. There are at present 3 silver clubs.

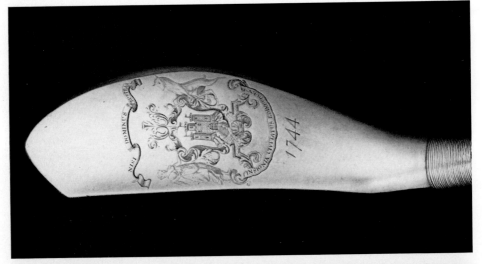

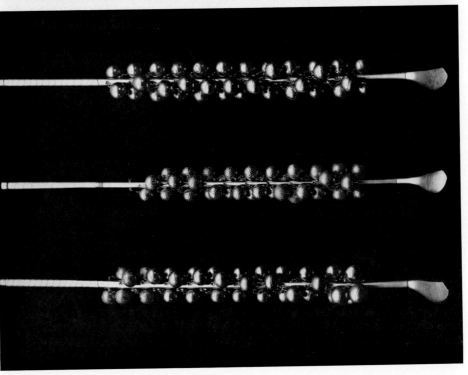

The Silver Clubs showing an engraved head and the balls attached

consented to come to Muirfield and give his expert advice. The conversation started on unpromising lines as the Secretary enquired whether Mr. Baxandall played golf. 'No, I am afraid I do not.' The Secretary was clearly perplexed: 'In that case, how do you pass the time?' Mr. Baxandall was, however, able to overcome this unexpected incredulity and confirm that the portrait, although not an inspiring one, was a genuine Raeburn. Alongside Inglis hangs the familiar portrait of John Taylor of the Exchequer (Captain on many occasions – 1807–8; 1814–15; 1823–25; 1828). He was painted by Sir John Watson Gordon, although there is an almost certainly apochryphal story that the kneeling figure of the caddie tee-ing his ball was painted by Raeburn. The evidence is, however, that Raeburn had died before the portrait was painted. Whoever the artist, he has done his job well, and Taylor remains for all to see as a round man, a man of substance and a player who would not willingly relinquish a winning lead.

Next follow two portraits from different eras. The first is of Alexander Stuart (Captain 1892–93), so far as is known the longest serving member of the Honourable Company – from 1876 to 1947. Although he is painted in his Captain's red coat, this contrives to avoid being a solemn portrait. The expression is extraordinarily life-like and members who look at it almost expect him to propose a match. Beside him hangs the agreeable likeness of Robert Maxwell (Captain 1912–13). Maxwell, as has been apparent from these pages, was for long a great figure at Muirfield, and the portrait, showing him in a moment of ease with the course as background, catches something of his powerful personality. Stanley Cursiter, the artist, has usually tended to favour a more ritual and elaborate approach and this informal likeness is one of his happiest achievements.

Rightly in pride of place above the chimneypiece hangs a copy of the portrait of William St. Clair of Roslin (Captain 1761–66 and 1770–71) painted by Sir George Chalmers, himself a member of the Honourable Company. St. Clair had been President of the Archers Council for ten years, from 1768 to 1778, and the original still hangs in Archers Hall. Most members would vote for St. Clair as the true epitome of the Muirfield man.

A genuflection to these portraits of the past, a glance at the original Rules of Golf (also framed on the wall) and into the dining-room. There, at the top table, the Silver Club lies, mace-like, as a symbol of the Captain's authority, along with the medals if it is a Medal Dinner. After a Lucullan feast as befits the solemnity of the occasion, the Loyal Toast is honoured and the winning scores at the last Medal competition are read out by the Secretary. The Captain invests the winners with their insignia; their health is drunk; and they make a commendably brief reply. Following a convenient interval, the serious business begins. The Book made at the last dinner may be read with the results of the matches played, sometimes to the discomfiture of those who have lost heavily or frequently. Then matches are proposed 'with the Captain's permission' on a named day (which must be adhered to) and for a given wager. This is expressed as 'Club stakes', consisting of a sovereign against each opponent, plus such modest addition as has been agreed by the contestants. Wagers will be laid vociferously by those who think they can detect the winning pair. When the Recorder has satisfied everyone that their bets are noted in the book the Captain calls the next member to propose a match. Eventually, some twenty-five or thirty games will be arranged for the period until the next dinner; the Recorder's health is toasted as a reward for his work; and the Honourable Company disperses long before the dead of the night's high noon when 'the welcome knell of the midnight bell rings forth its jolliest tune'.

The Honourable Company's trophies are generally of such antiquity that they deserve a closer look. By far the most valuable and unusual possessions are the silver clubs presented to the Honourable Company by the City of Edinburgh in 1744, 1811 and 1879 for annual competition, the winner becoming 'Captain of the Golf' for the following year. At the start, the Silver Club was awarded for the best score on the links on a specific day. It mattered not whether the winner was too imperious or, for that matter, too self-effacing to preside over the affairs of the Company; he still became Captain. It was not until 1836, on the move from Musselburgh, that the first Captain (Mr. William Wood) was elected. Since then, election has not been directly related to skilful performance on the course. To mark his tenure of office, the Captain attaches an inscribed silver ball to the club. On the first club there are forty-four balls; on the second, forty-five; and on the third, forty-three to date. The silver replicas themselves symbolise and summarise the development of golf since 1744. Up to 1865 the balls were of the old feathery type; for the next ten years they reproduce the hand-hammered gutta ball; then to the moulded gutta; the first Haskell in 1903; and balls more immediately recognisable as being like the ones used at present.

Apart from the Silver Club, the Club's oldest trophy is a cup authorised by Minute of 14th March, 1774:

> That there should annually be purchased out of the Company's funds a silver cup value £10 to be played for by the members; the winner of the cup to pay two guineas towards next year's cup and be barred from the cup afterwards.

Two cups still remain in the Club's possession – those won by Robert Annan in 1776 and by William Simpson in 1790. The cup was competed for until 1801 when it seems that the penalty for winning was reckoned too severe and affected the number of entries. The last winner was W. Oliphant. In 1790 the Honourable Company seem to have been – unusually for them – much concerned to improve the standard of play:

> As a spur to golfing, it is proposed that a gold medal, value about five guineas, should be played for and won by the winner for the year and the winner not to be excluded from playing for it again. The winner's name and year to be engraved on it.

A new medal was provided every year until 1828 when a larger one was produced and the winner had his name and score engraved on it, while he himself received a replica. The Gold Medal is played for on the first Saturday in May, and the present one is the seventh which the Club has produced. Inflation has, however, made it impossible to reward the winner with even a replica, and his only satisfaction is the entry of his name in the records. There is also an autumn gold medal and a silver medal (competed for at the Spring Meeting) given by Sir Walter Simpson (Captain 1887). This has an agreeable symmetrical design of crossed clubs round a ball which has been identified as being like an old 'Eclipse'. The Musselburgh medal, presented by members of the Club who had been at Loretto School, has embossed on it a likeness of the grandstand at Musselburgh where the members kept their clubs when they first moved there from Leith. The Grant Cup, presented by Lady Sybil Grant in memory of her husband, which is awarded for the best aggregate scores in the Spring and Autumn medal competitions, completes the tally. The Honourable Company deprecates handicap competitions; none are held.

The competition most enjoyed by the members is played for prizes of a very different order. In 1953 the Captain (C. J. Y. Dallmeyer) commented that, although New Year's day was sternly observed as a tribal holiday in Scotland, very little was done either to provide entertainment or to relieve excesses left over from Hogmanay. So he hit upon the highly original idea of the Captain's Frolic. It would be played every first of January: the rules would be as hilarious as possible: play in foursomes would be according to the Stableford system: and eighteen holes must be finished, but luncheon would be allowed after nine. Two further ordinances allowed the Captain to determine the partnerships (with benevolence or malice, as the humour moved him) and required all competitors to contribute a prize in kind – a bottle, or a brace of pheasant, or, in one year, a Stilton cheese disguised as a Christmas cake – so that all would return home rewarded.

From the start, the Frolic has provided a fine Muirfield day. The arrival of the tribesmen to greet old friends at the beginning of another year's golf is followed by just enough exercise appropriate to the day. After seasonable refreshments, the remaining holes are played and the dining-room fills with members ready to inspect the prizes laid out, sometimes wrapped to conceal their content, like a harvest festival. The names of the players according to their scores are read out by the Captain and they come forward to make their selection amid the shouts and comments of the assembly. So the prizes dwindle till all are taken and all the players rewarded. On one occasion, the Captain, in order to emphasise that this was primarily a social event and to punish cupidity, awarded the prizes in reverse order, the boobies being given the first choice. And for those who imagine that the ice-floes on the Firth of Forth do not begin to break till late Spring, only once has the Frolic been frustrated by adverse weather.

The picaresque tale of the Gentlemen Golfers is almost told. It is a story not confined to the golf actually played on the links at Leith, Musselburgh and Muirfield, although memorable rounds are embalmed in these pages. But stroke by stroke is the ultimate in boredom, only to be inflicted sadistically on one's enemies, and we have been more concerned with the attitudes, social, athletic or philosophical, of the members of the Honourable Company to each other and to the outside world.

Towards their fellows, the members cultivate a well-mannered, Augustan scepticism about their ability to play golf, to fix a match not loaded to their own advantage, or to make a wager which is exactly as it seems. Towards visitors they are like chameleons. The Olympians – the champions, actual and potential; the international competitors; the great names from the United States – are welcomed with proper deference.

The Bench and Bar are received with a mixture of apprehension and wonder. Can such kenspeckle sportsmen really represent the full majesty of the law? The Armed Services appear as former comrades; and the Senior Golfing Society reminds the members that, in time, only the soundest swing will withstand the erosion of age. Individuals come to have a day's healthful exercise and enjoyment, for that is what it is all about.

Now they stand perpetuated like the athletes on some ancient Attic frieze – addressing the ball with closed or open stance, conversing with their opponents or gesticulating to make some punitive point. Long may they continue, like the inhabitants of Homer's Syra, to enjoy the benefits of the old racecourse on the Hundred Acre Field –

Not over populated: fine for grazing cattle and sheep: rich too in wine and grain. No lack is felt here: no disease wars on its people: or ills that plague all men.

But, if this is too fanciful, there are two more realistic postscripts. The Senator of the College of Justice who is the Club's Senior Trustee will remind aspiring champions that his favourite shots are the practice swing and the conceded putt, and that the rest can never be mastered; and, when the last of the day's incredible shots has been distilled in a suitable spirit, Miss Straiton, to whom the members have paid their dues at her desk since she first joined the Honourable Company's staff forty years ago, will say, as she tidies up the last bills: 'It's been a nice day. I think that they have all enjoyed themselves.'

CAPTAINS

From 1744

1744–47 John Rattray	1791 James Dalrymple
1748 Hon. James Leslie	1792 John Trotter
1749 David Dalrymple	1793 George Cheape
1750 Hon. Francis Charteris	1794 and 1795 Robert Allan
1751 John Rattray	1796 John Gray
1752 Lord Drummore	1797 Sir James Stirling, Bt.
1753 Sir Henry Seton, Bt.	1798 Thomas Hay
1754 and 1755 W. Cross	1799 John Gray
1756 Sir Henry Seton, Bt.	1800 John Clerk
1757 Robert Clerk	1801 A. M. Guthrie
1758 Thomas Boswall	1802 Thomas Mure
1759 Andrew Hamilton	1803 and 1804 John Gray
1760 William Hog	1805 A. M. Guthrie
1761 William St. Clair of Roslin	1806 James Scott
1762 Sir R. Henderson, Bt.	1807 and 1808 John Taylor
1763 Col. Horn Elphinstone	1809 and 1810 George Mitchell
1764 Colin Campbell	1811 Birnie Brown
1765 Col. Horn Elphinstone	1812 Burnet Bruce
1766 William St. Clair of Roslin	1813 A. M. Guthrie
1767 William Hog	1814 and 1815 John Taylor
1768 Alexander Keith	1816 Col. R. Anstruther
1769 Thomas Stoddart	1817 and 1818 Walter Cook
1770 and 1771 William St. Clair of Roslin	1819 and 1820 John Mansfield
1772 James Rannie	1821 and 1822 George Ramsay
1773 Duncan McMillan	1823–25 John Taylor
1774 James Cheape	1826 and 1827 Henry M. Low
1775 Alexander Elphinstone	1828 John Taylor
1776 James Cheape	1829–35 Robert Menzies
1777 and 1778 John Trotter	1836 William Wood
1779 Sir Alexander Don, Bt.	1837 and 1838 John Mansfield
1780 Alexander Keith	1839–42 Thomas Paton
1781 Alexander Duncan	1843 and 1844 W. A. Cunningham
1782–84 William Inglis	1845–48 George Maclachlan
1785 Major George Hay	1849–51 Sir David Baird, Bt.
1786 Robert Allan	1852 W. M. Goddard
1787 and 1788 Lord Elcho	1853 and 1854 Ord Graham Campbell
1789 Thomas Mure	1855–58 Alexander Mackenzie
1790 William Simpson	1859 Robert Cowan

1860 and 1861	D. B. Wauchope
1862 and 1863	John Blackwood
1864	Gilbert Mitchell Innes
1865 and 1866	The Earl of Stair
1867	Sir Alexander Kinloch, Bt.
1868	Andrew Gillon
1869 and 1870	Capt. Alexander Lindsay
1871	Sir Hew Hume Campbell, Bt.
1872 and 1873	George Maclachlan
1874 and 1875	J. L. Mansfield
1876 and 1877	John Wharton Tod
1878 and 1879	W. J. Mure
1880 and 1881	B. Hall Blyth
1882 and 1883	Arthur Makgill
1884 and 1885	D. D. Whigham
1886 and 1887	Sir Walter G. Simpson, Bt.
1888 and 1889	James Syme
1890 and 1891	Col. J. W. H. Anderson
1892 and 1893	Alexander Stuart
1894 and 1895	A. Graham Murray
1896 and 1897	William Hope
1898 and 1899	G. F. Melville
1900 and 1901	Henry Cook
1902 and 1903	L. M. Balfour-Melville
1904 and 1905	J. E. Laidlay
1906 and 1907	A. R. Paterson
1908 and 1909	Patrick Murray
1910 and 1911	A. R. C. Pitman
1912 and 1913	Robert Maxwell
1914–18	C. J. G. Paterson
1919 and 1920	A. G. G. Asher
1921 and 1922	David Lyell
1923 and 1924	The Lord Kinross
1925 and 1926	Stair A. Gillon
1927 and 1928	R. K. Blair
1929 and 1930	A. W. Robertson Durham
1931 and 1932	John Cook
1933 and 1934	Sir John C. Couper
1935 and 1936	B. Hall Blyth
1937 and 1938	Hon. R. B. Watson
1939–41	R. H. Maconochie
1942–45	R. Y. Weir
1946 and 1947	J. A. Robertson Durham
1948 and 1949	R. M. McLaren
1950 and 1951	P. C. Smythe
1952 and 1953	C. J. Y. Dallmeyer
1954 and 1955	G. L. A. Jamieson
1956 and 1957	A. L. McClure
1958 and 1959	R. M. Carnegie
1960 and 1961	J. R. Watherston
1962 and 1963	G. T. Chiene
1964 and 1965	Hon. W. D. Watson
1965–67	Col. T. R. Broughton
1968 and 1969	T. R. Macgregor
1970 and 1971	Hon. Lord Robertson

RECORDERS
From 1783

1783–96 John Gray	1828–50 James Hay
1796–98 John Edgar and Thomas Duncan	1850–65 James Blackwood
1799 Thomas Duncan and D. Murray	1865–69 H. J. Wylie
	1869–76 J. Wharton Tod
1800 Archibald Gibson	1876–82 Henry Cook
1801–3 James Laidlaw and Alexander Lumsden	1882–88 James L. Mansfield
	1888–96 B. Hall Blyth
1803–6 Alexander Lumsden	1896–1910 R. H. Johnston
1806–9 Joseph Gordon	1910–19 T. M. Hunter
1809–11 Walter Cook	1919–24 H. D. Lawrie
1811–16 Adam Longmore	1924–32 William Robertson
1816–23 John Taylor	1932–46 R. M. McLaren
1823–26 Walter Cook	1947–55 I. H. Bowhill
1826–28 William Wood	1955–63 G. Robertson Durham
	1963– W. M. Miller

The Gold Medal

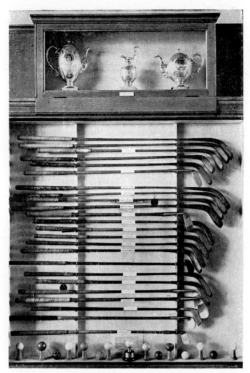

Ancient Clubs and Balls

The Smoking Room

WINNERS OF
THE CLUB GOLD AND SILVER MEDALS
From 1790

WINNERS OF THE GOLD MEDAL

Competed for on Leith Links
(Two rounds of 5 holes each)

Year		Year		Strokes
1790	Robert Allan	1812	Wm. Oliphant	
1792 Jan.	(after postponement from Dec. 1791) Robert Allan	1813	Wm. Mitchell	
		1814	Walter Cook	
1792 Dec.	Richard Stoddart	1815	Walter Cook	
1794 Feb.	Thomas Stoddart, Junior	1816	Wm. Mitchell	
		1817	Walter Cook	
1795 Jan.	Robert Allan	1818	Walter Cook	
1795 May	Robert Allan	1819	Wm. Mitchell	
1800	John Taylor	1820	Adam Longmore	
1801	Wm. Oliphant	1821	Alexander Mitchell	
1802	John Taylor	1822	Alexander Mitchell	
1803	Wm. Oliphant	1823	Alexander Mitchell	
1804	A. M. Guthrie	1824	Charles Shaw	*Strokes*
1805	John Taylor	1825	Charles Shaw	65
1806	John Taylor	1826	H. M. Low	60
1807	Walter Cook	1827	McGrieux (Samuel Messieux)	66
1808	Wm. Oliphant	1828	John Taylor	63
1809	Wm. Oliphant	1829*	John H. Wood	
1810	Wm. Oliphant	1830	John H. Wood	
1811	Wm. Oliphant			

* Competed for at Musselburgh.

Competed for at Musselburgh
(Two rounds of 8 holes each)

Year		Strokes	Year		Strokes
1836	William Wood	93	1853	John Bruce	90
1837	William Wood	87	1854	Capt. Campbell	84
1838	W. M. Goddard	85	1855	Robert Hay	81
1839	Thomas Patton	85	1856	W. M. Goddard	76
1840	James Skelton	88	1857	Robert Hay	84
1841	William Wood	85	1858	O. G. Campbell	86
1842	J. H. Dundas	85	1859	H. J. Wylie	90
1843	W. M. Goddard	85	1860	O. G. Campbell	88
1844	W. M. Goddard	87	1861	Gilbert M. Innes	80
1845	J. T. Gordon	99	1862	T. D. McWhannell	82
1846	W. M. Goddard	87	1863	O. G. Campbell	80
1847	O. G. Campbell	94	1864	H. J. Wylie	82
1848	Charles Cundell	88	1865	Gilbert M. Innes	83
1849	H. J. Wylie	86	1866	W. J. Mure	86
1850	Capt. Maitland, R.N.	81	1867	Gilbert M. Innes	80
1851	H. J. Wylie	83	1868	Robert Clark	81
1852	Capt. Maitland		1869	Gilbert M. Innes	75
	Dougall, R.N.	88			

Competed for at Musselburgh
(Two rounds of 9 holes each)

Year		Strokes	Year		Strokes
1870	Dr. Argyll Robertson	83	1881	W. J. Mure	87
1871	E. L. I. Blyth	87	1882	L. M. Balfour	81
1872	John Dun	84	1883	J. E. Laidlay	85
1873	E. L. I. Blyth	90	1884	L. M. Balfour	83
1874	Dr. Argyll Robertson	84	1885	James L. Mansfield	84
1875	Robert Clark	85	1886	L. M. Balfour	83
1876	Dr. Argyll Robertson	83	1887	J. E. Laidlay	79
1877	James L. Mansfield	84	1888	J. E. Laidlay	83
1878	Capt. A. M. Brown, R.N.	82	1889	L. M. Balfour	82
1879	W. J. Mure	82	1890	J. E. Laidlay	85
1880	W. J. Mure	86	1891	J. E. Laidlay	82

Competed for at Muirfield
Spring Meeting

Year		Strokes	Year		Strokes
1892	L. M. Balfour	79	1932	Abandoned	
1893	J. E. Laidlay	78	1933	W. A. Cochrane	80
1894	R. H. Johnston	79	1934	J. R. Pelham-Burn	78
1895	G. Gordon Robertson	83	1935	F. W. Paulin	79
1896	Major D. A. Kinloch	85	1936	I. H. Bowhill	76
1897	C. L. Dalziel	88	1937	Capt. W. L. Steele	77
1898	J. E. Laidlay	82	1938	W. I. E. Thorburn	77
1899	J. E. Laidlay	85	1939	I. A. D. Lawrie	77
1900	T. M. Hunter	79	1939–1945 World War		
1901	Robert Maxwell	80	1946	P. M. Smythe	80
1902	N. F. Hunter	79	1947	C. D. Lawrie	88
1903	Robert Maxwell	80	1948	Sqdn. Leader P. L. Arnott	76
1904	Robert Maxwell	78	1949	I. D. M. Considine	74
1905	G. F. Dalziel	85	1950	T. R. Macgregor	79
1906	C. L. Dalziel	80	1951	J. D. Tweedie	82
1907	J. E. Laidlay	82	1952	G. W. Mackie	76
1908	Capt. C. K. Hutchison	83	1953	I. D. M. Considine	77
1909	Robert Maxwell	80	1954	I. D. M. Considine	76
1910	Capt. C. K. Hutchison	76	1955	G. Robertson Durham	75
1911	J. E. Laidlay	78	1956	J. W. Draper	75
1912	Robert Maxwell	91	1957	J. W. Draper	77
1913	R. T. Boothby	79	1958	A. L. McClure	78
1914	Robert Maxwell	73	1959	P. R. Bryce	78
1915–1919 The Great War			1960	A. L. McClure	76
1920	A. Burn-Murdoch	86	1961	Major D. A. Blair	69
1921	L. M. Balfour-Melville	83	1962	Major D. A. Blair	70
1922	Robert Maxwell	80	1963	J. L. Mitchell	76
1923	G. B. Crole	79	1964	A. C. N. Ferguson	79
1924	F. W. Paulin	80	1965	G. Robertson Durham	77
1925	Douglas Currie	79	1966	R. H. J. Mackie	74
1926	Douglas Currie	73	1967	R. H. J. Mackie	72
1927	P. C. Smythe	77	1968	C. D. Lawrie	73
1928	W. Willis Mackenzie	79	1969	R. H. J. Mackie	76
1929	W. Willis Mackenzie	79	1970	A. R. McInroy	76
1930	F. W. Paulin	79	1971	J. G. Salvesen	75
1931	G. T. Chiene	76			

WINNERS OF THE WINTER MEDAL
(Gold)

Competed for at Musselburgh
(Two rounds of 9 holes each)

Year		Strokes	Year		Strokes
1871	G. Mitchell Innes	85	1882	L. M. Balfour	84
1872	G. Mitchell Innes	90	1883	W. J. Mure	84
1873	Dr. Argyll Robertson	84	1884	L. M. Balfour	82
1874	E. L. I. Blyth	84	1885	J. E. Laidlay	83
1875	W. J. Mure	80	1886	J. E. Laidlay	82
1876	Robert Clark	83	1887	J. E. Laidlay	80
1877	Robert Clark	86	1888	J. E. Laidlay	80
1878	John Wharton Tod	83	1889	L. M. Balfour	87
1879	E. L. I. Blyth	83	1890	J. E. Laidlay	83
1880	John Wharton Duff	86	1891	Alexander Stuart	80
1881	Alexander Stuart	83			

Competed for at Muirfield

Year		Strokes	Year		Strokes
1892	L. M. Balfour	81	1920	Robert Maxwell	79
1893	L. M. Balfour-Melville	86	1921	Robert Maxwell	82
1894	W. M. De Zoete	82	1922	Major C. K. Hutchison	80
1895	J. E. Laidlay	80	1923	Douglas Currie	82
1896	Major D. A. Kinloch	80	1924	G. B. Crole	80
1897	A. R. Paterson	81	1925	S. G. Rome	83
1898	L. M. Balfour-Melville	82	1926	F. W. Paulin	82
1899	J. E. Laidlay	86	1927	W. Willis Mackenzie	75
1900	J. E. Laidlay	84	1928	S. G. Rome	77
1901	Robert Maxwell	77	1929	W. Willis Mackenzie	79
1902	Robert Maxwell	79	1930	P. C. Smythe	78
1903	J. E. Laidlay	76	1931	I. H. Bowhill	77
1904	Robert Maxwell	76	1932	S. G. Rome	77
1905	J. E. Laidlay	75	1933	I. H. Bowhill	76
1906	Robert Maxwell	78	1934	I. A. D. Lawrie	75
1907	Capt. C. K. Hutchison	74	1935	J. N. Shaw	79
1908	T. M. Hunter	77	1936	S. G. Rome	78
1909	Robert Maxwell	82	1937	Capt. W. L. Steele	75
1910	L. M. Balfour-Melville	81	1938	J. T. Campbell	78
1911	Robert Maxwell	79	1939–45 World War		
1912	Capt. C. K. Hutchison	79	1946	I. H. Bowhill	79
1913	Capt. J. A. Orr	77	1947	C. J. Y. Dallmeyer	77
1914–1918 The Great War			1948	R. M. Carnegie	78
1919	Robert Maxwell	82	1949	G. Robertson Durham	76

Year		Strokes	Year		Strokes
1950	A. L. McClure	77	1961	Major D. A. Blair	74
1951	G. Robertson Durham	76	1962	R. H. J. Mackie	77
1952	R. M. Carnegie	73	1963	J. T. Williamson	81
1953	G. Robertson Durham	72	1964	J. M. Dykes	76
1954	G. W. Mackie	76	1965	A. C. N. Ferguson	76
1955	J. W. Draper	79	1966	G. Robertson Durham	79
1956	C. D. Lawrie	74	1967	J. G. Salvesen	78
1957	J. W. Draper	74	1968	I. S. Dougal	76
1958	J. W. St. C. Scott	75	1969	J. B. Cochran	73
1959	G. W. Mackie	72	1970	J. G. Salvesen	74
1960	J. M. Dykes	77	1971	R. P. White	75

WINNERS OF THE SILVER MEDAL

Spring Meeting
(presented by the Captain in 1887)

Competed for at Musselburgh
(Two rounds of 9 holes each)

Year		Strokes	Year		Strokes
1887	L. M. Balfour	83	1890	Robert Craig	86
1888	L. M. Balfour	85	1891	C. E. S. Chambers	84
1889	J. E. Laidlay	86			

Competed for at Muirfield

Year		Strokes	Year		Strokes
1892	J. E. Laidlay	80	1905	J. Younger, Junior	87
1893	R. H. Johnston	85	1906	J. E. Laidlay	83
1894	J. E. Laidlay	81	1907	Robert Maxwell	83
1895	Major D. A. Kinloch	85	1908	Robert Maxwell	84
1896	H. F. Caldwell	85	1909	Capt. C. K. Hutchison	84
1897	A. Stuart	88	1910	L. M. Balfour-Melville	76
1898	C. L. Dalziel	86	1911	Mark Tennant	78
1899	A. D. Blyth	86	1912	J. R. Gairdner	93
1900	C. L. Dalziel	82	1913	Robert Maxwell	80
1901	P. Balfour	80	1914	J. R. Gairdner	79
1902	W. H. Fowler	81	1915–1919	The Great War	
1903	J. E. Laidlay	86	1920	D. M. Wood	87
1904	J. E. Laidlay	78	1921	Robert Maxwell	84

K

Year		Strokes	Year		Strokes
1922	Douglas Currie	83	1950	I. D. M. Considine	79
1923	Douglas Currie	80	1951	M. M. Thorburn	82
1924	R. K. Blair	80	1952	D. S. Middleton	78
1925	F. W. Paulin	80	1953	G. Robertson Durham	77
1926	S. G. Rome	79	1954	J. H. Campbell	76
1927	W. Willis Mackenzie	78	1955	J. M. Dykes	77
1928	I. H. Bowhill	82	1956	J. M. Stewart	77
1929	F. W. Paulin	81	1957	J. M. Sturrock	78
1930	I. H. Bowhill	81	1958	G. Robertson Durham	79
1931	Major T. J. Mitchell	78	1959	Lt.-Col. A. M. M. Bucher	79
1932	Abandoned		1960	J. D. Tweedie	76
1933	James Haldane	80	1961	G. Robertson Durham	75
1934	F. W. Paulin	78	1962	G. Robertson Durham	76
1935	R. M. Carnegie	79	1963	A. R. McInroy	79
1936	S. G. Rome	78	1964	I. M. Robertson	80
1937	Major W. H. Callander	79	1965	C. N. Hastings	78
1938	R. M. Carnegie	80	1966	J. G. Salvesen	76
1939	G. T. Chiene	78	1967	W. B. M. Laird	75
1939–1945 World War			1968	R. P. White	78
1946	C. D. Lawrie	81	1969	I. W. H. Leslie	78
1947	G. Robertson Durham	90	1970	D. R. J. Stewart	77
1948	D. S. Middleton	79	1971	G. Robertson Durham	76
1949	A. L. McClure	77			

WINNERS OF
THE MUSSELBURGH (Silver) MEDAL

Autumn Meeting
Competed for at Muirfield

Year		Strokes	Year		Strokes
1908	J. E. Laidlay	77	1924	C. L. Dalziel	81
1909	Capt. C. K. Hutchison	85	1925	D. M. Wood	86
1910	Capt. C. K. Hutchison	83	1926	H. C. Stuart	85
1911	J. E. Laidlay	80	1927	A. W. Robertson Durham	79
1912	J. E. Laidlay	81	1928	C. J. Y. Dallmeyer	80
1913	Robert Maxwell	77	1929	R. A. Gallie	80
1914–1918 The Great War			1930	R. M. Carnegie	80
1919	J. E. Laidlay	84	1931	R. M. Carnegie	77
1920	Capt. C. K. Hutchison	81	1932	J. R. Pelham-Burn	78
1921	W. F. C. McClure	83	1933	R. M. Carnegie	76
1922	M. M. Thorburn	80	1934	R. M. McLaren	76
1923	A. Burn-Murdoch	84	1935	F. W. Paulin	79

Year		Strokes	Year		Strokes
1936	J. D. H. McIntosh	78	1957	A. R. McInroy	76
1937	G. T. Chiene	77	1958	P. R. Bryce	76
1938	P. J. Oliphant	79	1959	J. W. Draper	76
1939–1945	World War		1960	Lt.-Col. A. M. M. Bucher	79
1946	J. D. H. McIntosh	81	1961	J. M. Dykes	74
1947	G. Robertson Durham	78	1962	J. G. Salvesen	80
1948	I. D. M. Considine	79	1963	R. J. Normand	81
1949	R. M. Carnegie	77	1964	R. H. J. Mackie	76
1950	G. Robertson Durham	79	1965	R. H. J. Mackie	77
1951	J. M. Cowan	76	1966	J. G. Salvesen	80
1952	G. Robertson Durham	77	1967	G. Robertson Durham	78
1953	I. D. M. Considine	79	1968	R. P. White	77
1954	J. M. Dykes	78	1969	C. N. Hastings	76
1955	Alastair Walker	80	1970	W. B. M. Laird	76
1956	P. R. Bryce	78	1971	A. C. N. Ferguson	75

WINNERS OF THE GRANT CUP

(Best aggregate score of Spring & Autumn
Medal Competitions)

Year		Strokes	Year		Strokes
1954	I. D. M. Considine	159	1963	J. G. Salvesen	162
1955	G. Robertson Durham	157	1964	A. C. N. Ferguson	155
1956	P. M. Smythe	158	1965	G. Robertson Durham	158
1957	J. W. Draper	151	1966	J. G. Salvesen	156
1958	J. W. St. C. Scott	157	1967	R. H. J. Mackie	151
1959	G. W. Mackie	151	1968	R. P. White	155
1960	Lt.-Col. A. M. M. Bucher	157	1969	R. H. J. Mackie	154
1961	Major D. A. Blair	143	1970	J. B. Cochran	155
1962	G. Robertson Durham	157	1971	R. P. White	152

AMATEUR CHAMPIONSHIPS AT MUIRFIELD
From 1897

British Amateur Championship

1897	A. J. T. Allan beat James Robb	4/2
1903	R. Maxwell beat H. G. Hutchinson	7/5
1909	R. Maxwell beat Capt. C. K. Hutchison	1 up
1920	C. J. H. Tolley beat R. A. Gardner, USA	at 37th
1926	Jesse Sweetser, USA beat A. F. Simpson	6/5
1932	J. de Forest beat E. W. Fiddian	3/1
1954	D. W. Bachli, Australia beat W. C. Campbell, USA	2 up

Scottish Amateur Championship

1923	J. T. Dobson beat W. W. Mackenzie	3/2
1928	W. W. Mackenzie beat W. E. Dodds	5/3
1938	E. D. Hamilton beat R. Rutherford	4/2
1949	R. Wight beat H. McInally	1 up
1955	R. R. Jack beat A. C. Miller	2/1
1962	S. W. T. Murray beat R. D. B. M. Shade	2/1
1968	G. B. Cosh beat R. L. Renfrew	4/3

Scottish Open Amateur Stroke Play Championship

1967	B. J. Gallacher	291

OPEN CHAMPIONSHIPS AT MUIRFIELD
From 1892

1892	Mr. H. H. Hilton, Royal Liverpool	305
1896	H. Vardon, Ganton (after a tie with J. H. Taylor, Winchester)	316
1901	James Braid, Romford	309
1906	James Braid, Walton Heath	300
1912	E. Ray, Oxhey	295
1929	Walter Hagen (USA)	292
1935	A. Perry, Leatherhead	283
1948	T. H. Cotton, Royal Mid Surrey	284
1959	G. J. Player, South Africa	284
1966	Jack Nicklaus (USA)	282

1929

W. Hagen, USA	75	67	75	75 =	292
J. Farrell, USA	72	75	76	75 =	298
L. Diegel, USA	71	69	82	77 =	299
Abe Mitchell, St. Albans	72	72	78	78 =	300
P. Alliss, GB	69	76	76	79 =	300
R. Cruickshank, USA	73	74	78	76 =	301

1935

Alfred Perry, Leatherhead	69	75	67	72 =	283
Alfred Padgham, Sundridge	70	72	74	71 =	287
Charles Whitcombe, Crews Hill	71	68	73	76 =	288
Bert Gadd, Braid Hills	72	75	71	71 =	289
Mr. W. Lawson Little, USA	75	71	74	69 =	289
H. Picard, USA	72	73	72	75 =	292

1948

T. H. Cotton, Royal Mid Surrey	71	66	75	72 =	284
F. J. Daly, Balmoral	72	71	73	73 =	289
N. J. von Nida, Australia	71	72	76	71 =	290
R. de Vicenzo, Argentine	70	73	72	75 =	290
J. Hargreaves, Sutton Coldfield	76	68	73	73 =	290
C. H. Ward, Little Aston	69	72	75	74 =	290

1959

G. J. Player, South Africa	75	71	70	68 = 284
F. Van Donck, Belgium	70	70	73	73 = 286
F. Bullock, Prestwick St. Ninians	68	70	74	74 = 286
S. S. Scott, Roehampton	73	70	73	71 = 287
C. O'Connor, Royal Dublin	73	74	72	69 = 288
Mr. R. R. Jack, Dullatur	71	75	68	74 = 288
S. L. King, Knole Park	70	74	68	76 = 288
J. Panton, Glenbervie	72	72	71	73 = 288

1966

J. Nicklaus, USA	70	67	75	70 = 282
D. Thomas, Dunham Forest	72	73	69	69 = 283
D. Sanders, USA	71	70	72	71 = 283
G. J. Player, South Africa	72	74	71	69 = 286
B. Devlin, Australia	73	69	74	70 = 286
K. Nagle, Australia	72	68	76	70 = 286
P. Rodgers, USA	74	66	70	76 = 286

INTERNATIONAL MATCHES AT MUIRFIELD

Walker Cup: British Isles v. USA
1959   Won by USA   9–3

FOURSOMES

R. R. Jack & D. N. Sewell	0	E. H. Ward & F. M. Taylor	1 up
J. B. Carr & G. B. Wolstenholme	0	W. Hyndman & T. D. Aaron	1 up
M. F. Bonallack & A. H. Perowne	0	C. R. Coe & W. J. Patton	9/8
M. S. R. Lunt & A. E. Shepperson	0	J. W. Nicklaus & H. W. Wettlaufer	2/1
	—		—
	0		4

SINGLES

J. B. Carr (2/1)	1	C. R. Coe	0
G. B. Wolstenholme	0	E. Harvey Ward (9/8)	1
R. R. Jack (5/3)	1	W. J. Patton	0
D. N. Sewell	0	W. Hyndman (4/3)	1
A. E. Shepperson	1	T. D. Aaron	0
M. F. Bonallack	0	D. R. Beman (2 up)	1
M. S. R. Lunt	0	H. W. Wettlaufer (6/5)	1
W. D. Smith	0	J. W. Nicklaus (5/4)	1
	—		—
	3		5

TOTAL   3–9 to USA

Home Amateur Internationals

1926	England	9 matches	Scotland	5	
1948	England	8	Scotland	2	(5 halved)
	England	8	Wales	6	(1 halved)
	England	8	Ireland	7	
	Ireland	10	Scotland	4	(1 halved)
	Ireland	11	Wales	1	(3 halved)
	Scotland	11	Wales	4	
1956	Scotland	10	Wales	4	(1 halved)
	Scotland	7	Ireland	6	(2 halved)
	Scotland	8	England	4	(3 halved)
	England	11	Ireland	4	
	England	10	Wales	4	(1 halved)
	Wales	8	Ireland	5	(2 halved)

LADIES COMPETITIONS AT MUIRFIELD

Scottish Ladies Championship
1914   Miss E. R. Anderson beat Miss F. S. Teacher at 20th hole

Vagliano Cup – British Isles v. Europe
1963   Won by British Isles   20–10

Curtis Cup – British Isles v. USA
1952   Won by British Isles   5–4

RECORD SCORES ROUND MUIRFIELD

As minor alterations to the course have been made before nearly every Open Championship (new tees, bunkers, etc), the best score at each by Amateur and Professional players respectively has become the record for the time being.

Since 1929, however, the tees off which members have played for the Spring and Autumn Meetings have remained practically the same.

Off the Medal tees the measurements of the holes are as follows:

Holes	Length (yds.)	Holes	Length (yds.)
1	429	10	475
2	363	11	363
3	385	12	385
4	187	13	154
5	516	14	462
6	473	15	407
7	187	16	198
8	451	17	528
9	495	18	429
Out	3,486	In	3,401
		Out	3,486
		Total	6,887 yds.

The present record Medal score is 69 by Major D. A. Blair in 1961. The details were:

```
3 4 3 3 4 4 2 5 4 = 32 Out ⎫
5 5 4 3 5 4 3 4 4 = 37 In  ⎬ 69
                            ⎭
```

BIBLIOGRAPHY

Golfing. W. & R. Chambers. 1887.

The Art of Golf. Sir Walter Simpson. 1890.

Golf in the Badminton Library. 1890.

Golf: A Royal and Ancient Game. Robert Clark, FRSE, FSAScot. Macmillan, 1893 (first edition privately 1875).

The Golf Book of East Lothian. Rev. John Kerr, MA, FRSE, FSAScot. Constable, 1896.

The Early Days of the Hon. Company of Edinburgh Golfers (1744 to 1764). C. B. Clapcott. 1938. Private.

The Honourable Company of Edinburgh Golfers on Leith Links (1744 to 1836). C. B. Clapcott. 1939. Private.

The Honourable Company of Edinburgh Golfers 1744–1944. R. M. McLaren. 1944. Private.

Some Comments on the Articles and Laws in playing the Golf. C. B. Clapcott. 1945. Private.

The Honourable Company of Edinburgh Golfers: Muirfield 1891–1914. Stair A. Gillon. 1946. Private.

A History of Golf in Britain. Cassell, 1952.

James Braid. Bernard Darwin. Hodder & Stoughton, 1952.

A History of Golf. Robert Browning, MA, LL.B. Dent, 1955.

The Story of the R. & A. J. B. Salmond. Macmillan, 1956.

St. Andrews Home of Golf. James K. Robertson. 'Citizen Office', St. Andrews, 1967.

Memorials of My Time. Lord Cockburn. Robert Grant, 1946 (original edition 1856).

The Expedition of Humphry Clinker. Tobias Smollett. Oxford University Press, 1930 (original edition 1771).

MU

379
3

yards

INDEX

Note : Names appearing only in the Foreword or Appendices and references to Muirfield and the Honourable Company are not indexed.

MR. JOHN TAYLOR
CAPTAIN OF THE HONOURABLE COMPANY OF EDINBURGH GOLFERS
Oil painting by Sir John Watson Gordon

THE FIRST LORD MACDONALD OF THE ISLES AS A BOY
WITH HIS BROTHER SIR JAMES MACDONALD OF SLEAT
Oil painting by an unknown artist of the eighteenth century